PI

CITIZEN MANUAL 2
RECONNAISSANCE

Published by
The Professional Citizen Project

Jack Morris

For my Family; I love you knuckleheads with all my heart. I could not do this without you.

Citizen Manual 2
Reconnaissance

Copyright © 2023 by The Professional Citizen
Project

ISBN: 979-8-9895092-1-8

Printed in the USA

www.ProCitizenProject.com

Contents

Contents   Page

THE PROFESSIONAL CITIZEN PROJECT

Thank you for your support for the Professional Citizen Project. The CM-1 manual launched us on this mission and set the bar incredibly high for the project. Writing the next follow-on manual has been a rewarding but challenging task. I knew the second in the series had to deliver; our community would expect the CM-2 to continue the high standards for The Project. After 12+ months of writing, re-writing, and re-writing again I am confident this reference will exceed your expectations. My sincere thanks to you for continuing this journey with us.

Sincerely

Introduction

Why the Professional Citizen Series of References?

Sorting through the massive amount of tactics and preparedness information is overwhelming. Content watchers (and even students at some classes) were fed an unending stream of irrelevant tactical and technical skills. The normal US mom, dad, wife, husband, sister, son, etc were (mostly) treated as an afterthought, left with no real way to sort through the mess and find a starting point. Available print references were in a similar state, many focused on executing tasks with a government level equipped force...or digging a bunker out in the back 40. There were alternatives, however none were squarely focused on translating military tactics and techniques directly to applicable Citizen requirements.

This series of manuals was developed from the need to provide a Citizen centric solution; a comprehensive series of references that is focused and built specifically for your use.

What is the Professional Citizen Reference Series?

The Professional Citizen series of references is a clearly written, easy to use set of references that address baseline individual tasks through complex small unit tactics - all done from the Citizen perspective.

Our community uses US military tactics as the starting point because they are both proven and the most available resource for us. The challenge with these sources is they are for a system built for a non-resource constrained organization (the military). The methods and associated resources far outstretch what we as Citizens can muster. The Professional Citizen series of manuals does not include irrelevant items such as conducting air assaults, loading helicopters, or emplacing cratering charges. The CM manuals provide information that is relevant to you; referencing only those tasks directly related to anticipated Citizen missions.

This series is grounded in proven Tactics, Techniques, and Procedures (TTPs) and doctrine. Some content is a direct lift from current doctrine because a particular subject or reference did not require adjustment. We also reached back into past doctrine as well. The official military doctrine development cycle is not always correct, sometimes the previous approaches are more effective (and less convoluted) than the new versions so don't get excited when you see terms or concepts that are recognizably "old". If we choose to use it rest assured that it works and is the better solution.

This Manual, Reconnaissance

The CM-2 is for the individual who has fully grasped and practiced the individual foundational tasks and concepts in CM-1. This manual is a balance of individual and leader tasks, dismounted reconnaissance fundamentals, as well as some introductory planning and mission analysis discussion. While most of the info in this manual is foundational and introductory, some of it can be challenging as you introduce yourself to new concepts. No worries, it will all come together and make sense as you practice and immerse yourself in the processes and internalize the tactics and concepts. Don't trip yourself up by thinking in terms of "advanced" as these concepts and skills are more building blocks to add to the basic requirements outlined in CM-1. The material in this manual is somewhat abbreviated and deliberately summarizes some details vs presenting a mass of relevant (but undigestible) information on the topics. These are the next logical steps to build on the CM-1 foundational skills and tactics. CM-2 is for the individual, small units, and the leaders who are willing and capable of putting their ruck on and conducting recon and security missions. You may be on your own, in a team, or assisting friendly US forces dealing with a tactical problem. To do so you will need a basic understanding of mission planning, organizing for combat, and reconnaissance. Post event conditions of a threat entity occupying US soil are almost unthinkable, but it is this very future we must consider and prepare for. The dismounted tactics and solutions contained in CM-2 will also apply to any local or regional kinetic event; training yourself and your group to address the worst-case scenario of a hostile occupation force puts you on solid footing to deal with any of the lesser crisis scenarios as well. The organization, tactics, and equipment recommendations in the CM-2 are just that; these are recommendations or "A way" of doing things. As with all our references we provide proven tactics and techniques, but these may not fit your use case exactly. You will adjust and apply these techniques to address your conditions and meet *your* requirements. This is the essence of the Professional Citizen series of manuals, applying your requirements to this framework will result in effective tactical SOPs for you and your group. The CM-2 does not re-state or review all the basic tasks from CM-1, this manual (CM-2) presumes familiarity and proficiency of those tasks by the reader. Use this reference to grow your skills to be capable of assisting US military, state, or local authorities during an inevitable crisis. An incident commander during a severe weather event will be grateful to have you or your group step up and volunteer to assist running a command post, managing assets, or providing information to shape the response to help your community. ***Do what works for you and your group; don't train from a place of fear that a particular method will not be legitimate because it does not look exactly like doctrine or someone else's tactics.***

The CM-2 is centered on recon (and some security tasks) at squad and below. It is our assessment that most of us in the community currently train in team or squad / heavy squad size elements, so we have written this to meet the community where it is. The opportunity to train in full platoon size or larger elements may be rare for you and your group during the pre-event period due to personnel availability and group numbers. If you are fortunate to have a larger group to habitually train together this manual still provides a great baseline of knowledge for your teams and squads. Organizations during a crisis will morph over time and get much larger, the reality is most of us can only gather a fire team or squad size element to train with on a regular basis during pre-X Hour "normal" times. A well-trained squad capable of operating independently can eventually integrate into part of a larger organization. This will go a long way toward building combat power for a regional partisan force.

Citizens Using Dismounted Guerilla Tactics

A Pro Citizen using guerilla or commando-like tactics, techniques, and procedures does not pretend to be anything other than what they are. This is not to say that a well-disciplined, well-trained group of Citizens cannot achieve an incredibly high level of proficiency (within reason due to the taxpayer funded enablers available to a state supported organized force). Applying the tactical concepts, high physical fitness standards, and the required discipline simply makes for a more capable, better trained, more physically fit Citizen. The tenets and principles used to develop professional soldiers can be applied to our use case as members of our communities; teams who are accustomed to working together and solving problems are an incredible asset during a crisis. This isn't always about conducting raids; manning command posts, conducting recons to check river levels or road status, and delivering firewood to stranded community members is also served by your training and preparation. This reference is for the individual who is ready to advance to the next level of tactical training; one who is willing to put in the work and perform at a level above and beyond the baseline requirements.

4

Attributes

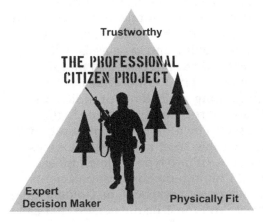

These are ever present, no matter what role you have in your community or group. You will recognize these from CM-1, these attributes apply to any and all individuals in this endeavor. The Professional Citizen values preparedness, physical fitness, training, and prides themselves on being proficient with all the relevant tools at their disposal. He or she has developed and practiced critical thinking skills to make decisions under extreme pressure with minimal information and time. He has the requisite skills that will be called upon in a crisis and has placed value on imparting that knowledge and mindset to his family, group, and community. He takes this responsibility seriously and builds his life around it; it is a way of life. This is a lifestyle that does not have to consume all of one's resources, the principles can be followed and implemented while maintaining a very "normal" financial life. The Pro Citizen is self-aware and knows his blind spots; he seeks out training and self-improvement to fill in those knowledge gaps. He is a member of a community and is part of a team; either as a member, organizer, or as a leader. He trains individually and as part of that team. He does not have a lone wolf mentality, nor does he see his role as only active if there is a widespread kinetic event. Power outages, adverse weather events, any disruptions of normality that impact his community members...all of these are events when he will step up to help his neighbors.

Trust. Trust is the basis for any great organization. We can train members past almost any deficiency if they are grounded in traditional values and morals, honorable, have integrity, and can be counted on when things are hard. Groups can train decision making and even assist with overcoming fitness shortfalls, but integrity and morals must be part of the character. Trust issues may not be apparent until a tough training cycle, look for indicators early and often. Odds are there is more than one high-performing special "I used to be a" in your community with great skills but has inexcusable trust and integrity issues. Don't be fooled by a resume of *any* type. Being honest, owning mistakes during training, meeting commitments, and treating other members with respect (the Golden Rule) are all indicators of trust. You must be the person that can be counted on to drive on and perform when they are cold, wet, and tired. Being tactically proficient with tons of real-world experience does not equate to trustworthiness. Choose carefully who you listen to, follow, or allow on your team and immediately remove a member that shows even the slightest integrity issue.

Expert Decision Maker. Decision making is the cornerstone of all tactical operations. From mundane micro decisions to complex mission planning and execution. The ability to make sound decisions in a timely manner can be trained and developed, but there is a "common sense" starting point that must be present in a team member. From the point man who must make split second decisions to the patrol leader who must lead under fire, all members must be capable of sound decisions. Not everyone is cut out to be a leader, but everyone must be able to make decisions at some level. Citizens will make decisions that affect not only them but the entire team. Being a person who can do so is an incredible asset for the group. The follow on to this concept is leaders for the organization will come from within; selecting a new team member is a vote for future consideration in a leadership position.

Physical Fitness. Out of shape people are combat ineffective before the fight ever starts. There is a considerable physical fitness obligation that comes with being in a patrol, one that cannot be trained or "caught up" after X Hour. Fit people stay healthier, stay awake longer on patrol, work harder, think clearer and perform better under stress. A team member must be able to pull their weight and keep up physically. Just like any other unit there will be individuals that excel in all things physical. If you are in a leadership position, make sure that the unit PT (physical training) standards are attainable, repeatable, and reasonable. There is always a bottom cutoff of "good enough" in any organization. From GSG9, Ranger Regiment, or SEAL Team 6, there are active team members that are only considered "good enough" when held against the organization's standards. The lower acceptable standard in those units is much higher than in regular organizations; it is all relative. It is a matter of setting and enforcing high minimum standards based on your group's requirements. These cannot be arbitrarily set to align with the fastest, strongest athlete on the team, they must be benchmarked against real requirements. Base your physical standards on your anticipated real-world mission set and it will result in a physically capable, cohesive team. By necessity the physical standards for fighters must be set at a level that some will not be able to achieve. The physical fitness standards you set for fighters in your group are not an exercise in inclusivity; there will be great Americans who will not be able to achieve the baseline requirements and that is OK. There may be incredible technical talent in your available group, but if the high-speed drone operator can't hump his own ruck or if there is a squad member who habitually fails time standards on training runs they should be assigned a different support role in the group / community. As stated in CM-1 *there is talent in every group, you must figure out where to allocate it.*

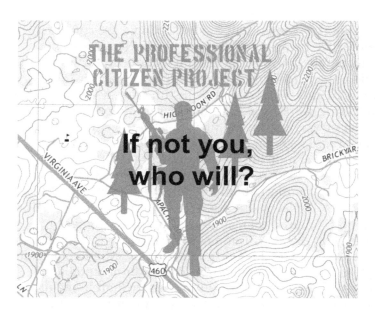

What tactical tasks can we expect to be called upon to do during a security crisis / kinetic event?

Mission Profile. We always reinforce the fact that odds are far greater that we will be pressed into service for some community crisis or neighbor event than responding to an invasion or war on US soil. Do you know exactly what will happen? No. None of us do. But we must start somewhere and hedge our bets by training and preparing in ways that will cover as many potential challenges as possible (in general terms). While tactical requirements in a regional or large-scale kinetic event are far less likely than a local environmental or weather crisis, the preparation and execution requirements described in this manual are far more complicated than being ready for the typical power outage. This complexity is the very reason why you must allocate time and effort to train for these missions. The larger categories of this mission set for us will most likely include unconventional/guerilla versions of conducting Reconnaissance (Recon) operations, performing Security operations specifically neighborhood and "property

8

patrols", conducting limited Attacks in the form of Ambushes, Sabotage, limited Raids, and Defending. Of these four, Reconnaissance and Security (R&S) will most likely be the backbone or foundation of any Citizen mission. The execution of R&S provides information and can create time and space to adjust to changing situations. For example, recon efforts will support decisions to transition from defense (security) of your homestead, neighborhood, or sanctuary to offensive or sabotage operations to protect the community and support friendly US forces. These skills directly translate and support your execution of community and property patrols and general security tasks for your homestead or local area. *Again, we don't want to view training these tasks only in anticipation of some wartime Red Dawn fantasy. This is a means to train in a way that will still serve you and your team for the more likely "lesser" events. Events requiring establishment of local security to stop looters or as an extra layer of enhanced neighborhood watch if there is a crisis.* Citizens organized in scout teams can provide the main force, homestead, or neighborhood critical information and early warning of threat activities to afford them enough time to prepare or maneuver their forces into ambush sites and blocking positions. Citizens in the Scout role will enable leaders to determine enemy intent, their willingness to fight, and identify weak points in the occupying force's logistics. Your team may help confirm or deny assumptions about the enemy, terrain, or the changing political / civil situation for the community leader, friendly US force, or yourself. You may conduct reconnaissance missions to provide information to be processed into actionable intelligence for local, regional, or military leaders.

As a crisis expands you may provide information in support of friendly US force attacks on the enemy or gather information that drives coordinated guerilla missions. Depending on the technology infrastructure and state of the country/region you may very well be the primary source of information for local leaders. Tasks could vary from looking for a new water source (water will be a far greater problem than most realize) to tracking an enemy battalion moving through your area. Reconnaissance by itself is never decisive, the guerilla force will also be required to conduct appropriate levels of direct action to have the desired effect on the enemy (we will address these operations in future manuals). The more combat power the threat allocates to protect these assets the less he has available to use against you and the friendly US forces in your area. You may be required to conduct counter insurgency tasks to find, fix, and destroy insurgent cells that were infiltrated across a porous border and have now activated against the US in a post X Hour scenario. The possibilities are endless...but none are in the category of large regular force actions for us.

During high threat conditions you, your family, or your team may be pressed to conduct offensive operations, just understand when doing so the chance of becoming decisively engaged by the enemy increases - and so does the risk. The imperative for the guerilla force is still to remain elusive / undetected and not become decisively engaged unless there is an overwhelming possibility of success. Hit and run tactics, sabotage, making enemy widows, breaking the morale of threat forces, and then quickly melting away into the terrain or community are the tactics of the guerilla force. The Pro Citizen (even in larger scale operations as a kinetic crisis expands) is neither equipped nor capable of sustained conventional combat operations against a larger / superior force. The cost of prolonged direct fire contact is too great for the force to bear, there are no replacements. Stealth, small unit and team movements, and an aversion to becoming decisively engaged are how we must view any future fight with a regular or organized force that threatens the US or our communities. Maintaining speed, agility, stealth and elusiveness must be ever present in a guerilla force.

Lethal Nerds. Current generation warfare is a mix of enablers that were once reserved for organized, state-sponsored militaries. These capabilities cannot be learned or caught back up easily, your team members that have these skills must be in place time now. Electronic warfare, cyber, and unmanned systems are all capabilities that can and will be leveraged by guerilla forces. Cyber experts, radio geeks, drone operators and intel folks can make or break your missions. The guerilla force must have these capabilities built in to be successful. Working with friendly conventional forces your combat nerds can provide critical information that can have strategic impact. Even in the scenarios of lesser severity (regional lawlessness, riots etc) having tech savvy team members that can radio direction find a roving criminal gang element and subsequently exploit the captured electronics can be a huge win for the friendly forces. Finding and developing this talent prior to X Hour is critical for the guerilla force.

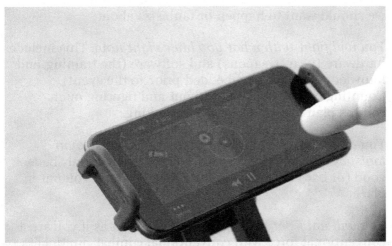

Lethal Nerds. Having experts that are all about the technology is an imperative in 5th Generation warfare. It isn't just radios and drones, understanding cyber and electronic signature risks and knowing how to exploit threat weaknesses is a high value skill. Find your nerds and welcome them in your team with open arms.

The Unsupported and Unfamiliar Ecosystem

Regional WROL, a civil war, invasion, or occupation of US soil by forces hostile to Citizens has a spot in the unimaginable category for most Americans. However, it carries the greatest risk and the most dangerous consequences of any possible scenario for our society and way of life (arguably this is closer to being a probability than at any other time during our lives). A role inside of this will require checking normal mode bias at the door; the faster you recognize the change and accept the fact that life will never be the same again the better. There are imperatives that the externally unsupported fighter must wrap their head around, among these imperatives are:

This is not a game, it is not apocalypse porn. Beware potential team members who think otherwise and guard your own thoughts against these ideas. If and when this comes to our soil it will be horrible; this is not something we should want to happen or fantasize about.

You will fight with what you have right now. This includes hardware (gear, weapons) and software (the training and knowledge you have embedded prior to the event). Counting on belt-feds lying about and figuring out a comms plan in stride is wishful thinking.

You and your group / local network are your own logistics system. The support you receive will only be as good (or bad) as the means and methods that you put in place.

You will not fight "as if". You will not fight as if you are a conventional force with conventional combat multipliers or assets, nor will you use conventional tactics. History is loaded with examples of unconventional forces that attempted to adopt the tactics of their conventional foes. To put it bluntly, it did not go well. Embrace perceived disadvantages and make them your strengths.

The Framework of the Future

The details of a possible (probable?) scenario that brings an external state sponsored organized threat into our communities is vague at best, but you must consider it in detail. This isn't meant to come across as "preachy" or the typical internet hyperbole, quite the opposite. We must consider this in real terms. It seems almost an impossible scenario as we think through this in our comfortable American minds, but if you are reading this you consider a future widespread crisis a possibility.

A modern city devolved. Sarajevo was transformed in short order from a modern thriving city to a killing ground. How would this play out in your community?

Envisioning a generic crisis scenario gives context for the training and operational requirements for this manual. This is not a guerilla warfare reference per se, it simply provides the backdrop for us to build this manual for you and provides ideas to support your training in context. Family and Group leaders must do detailed studies (Intelligence Preparation of the Battlefield or IPB) to build understanding of their area. These studies of your extended local area (also known as the Operational

Environment (OE)) inform your plans for your specific terrain and conditions. Even with an incredibly large set of planning assumptions due to all the unknowns we must start somewhere. It is easy to become numbed into inaction by the uncomfortable filling in of all these unknowns. Not only is it OK to assume some things for planning purposes; assumptions are a *necessity* during your analysis. These assumptions fill in the missing pieces to allow you to continue planning. These are not wild guesses. Planning assumptions are logical, probable (sometimes only possible) pieces of data that you deliberately think through. For example, you might assume a conventional enemy will identify the

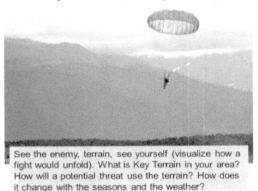

See the enemy, terrain, see yourself (visualize how a fight would unfold). What is Key Terrain in your area? How will a potential threat use the terrain? How does it change with the seasons and the weather?

crossroads in your North Carolina Mountain town as Key Terrain and will try to seize it. You make this assumption since the routes connect three existing larger cities/towns and there are no other high-speed avenues through the mountain passes that bypass it. That assumption will influence your plan as well as your training. If you are incorrect and this assumption eventually proves to be false it is no big deal, you adjust your plan. Even if you are only 10 percent correct in your initial assessment and planning you will still be in a 100 percent better position since you have already thought deliberately through the problem. This is the real value, the methodical mental process of thinking through the components. How do you assess it will play out? What will your family, group, or unit be required to plan for? What tasks do you need to train to be ready? There are more questions than answers, but that is the nature of this business.

Chapter 1
Squad Organization

Leadership

Leadership is the core of all organizations; it is the most essential element of combat power that will make or break a team. We will briefly touch on the details of small unit leadership, other CM references in the series will eventually address the subject in depth. Small unit leadership is ultimately about one thing—leading fighters to accomplish the mission. This process starts during training and when forming your group. Leaders motivate people to pursue actions, focus thinking, manage violence, and shape decisions for the greater good of the organization and the mission. Citizen leaders will be especially challenged due to the lack of formal organization (perceived or actual), and the absence of decades of tradition and institutional systems that exist in standing armies. Without leadership, groups of well-intentioned Citizens are nothing more than an undirected mob.

Leaders need and must provide:
Purpose: the *reason* to accomplish the mission.
Direction: the *means* to accomplish the mission.
Motivation: the *will* to accomplish the mission.

Leaders use Command and Control (C2) to influence their subordinates to accomplish the mission.

Command is the authority leaders exercise over individuals in their group by virtue of their position. For informal volunteer organizations this authority is derived through the organization itself. Positions are only as solid as the group deems it to be; a billet alone is not basis for authority as an irregular force leader. The nature of a Citizen organization does not lend itself to doing so. Don't misunderstand this point, these positions must be well defined and respected or the unit will be a collection of "I

15

disagree so I'll do what I want to" mob. The assigned leadership position in and of itself is not the basis of authority. In non-traditional organizations the selected person's competence solidifies legitimacy for the position, not the reverse.

Control is the direction and guidance of subordinates to ensure accomplishment of the mission. Leadership is the art of exercising C2 to influence and direct people in such a way as to obtain their willing obedience, confidence, respect, and loyalty to accomplish the mission. Leadership is the most vital component of C2.

Leadership involves a combination of character and professional competence. Leading in combat is the guerilla leader's most important challenge. These are not strangers being sent out to conduct dangerous recon or sabotage missions. They are your neighbors, friends - even your sons and daughters. Selecting and training your group's leaders that will make these decisions is beyond critical. We highly recommend selecting, assessing, and training these team members as soon as possible. If you are leading your family unit, this responsibility falls squarely on your shoulders.

Leadership positions must be filled before an event occurs. Unity of command requires that two leaders, whether formal or informal, may not exercise the same command relationship over the same unit at any one time. Power struggles are counterproductive and unnecessary. This concept must be maintained all the way down at the fire team and squad levels; having a "no, I'm in charge...no I am" situation in an element (eg fighting for control of a squad or platoon) is unacceptable.

The leadership / command structure in a tactical formation exists to allow leaders to maintain a manageable span of control (3 to 5 people). At each level there are distinct responsibilities and authority, these must be maintained and bought into by any volunteer. The organizational concept applies for followers as well, a team member who is unwilling to follow direction from an emplaced leader during training or the "good times" is a liability and should be considered for removal from the group. Conversely a leader who habitually makes poor decisions in training should be moved to a new position that matches their knowledge, skills, and abilities. As the theater matures during a crisis or invasion the leadership will become even more informal as the guerilla force grows. This is somewhat counter-intuitive, but the fire team and squads you have formed and trained with pre–X Hour will likely have the most formal leadership structures. As larger groups form during a crisis and actions of various groups are coordinated, informal leaders will emerge from the community and region.

Leaders are *not* there to primarily be trigger-pullers. Yes, they must be very proficient at doing so, but their role is to lead. They (or you) are in a leadership position because they understand situations quickly and apply combat power at the right place and time. They must not get sucked so far into the fight that they do not see the interrelationship of their unit, the enemy, and the terrain. They must be able to control the tempo of missions and have a "feel" for their subordinates; they know when to push them and when they need rest. Leaders are the voice of reason and morality when emotions run high. Leaders head off poor choices that can do strategic damage to the entire cause.

Leaders don't lead by checklists. As stated earlier this is not a leadership specific manual so we have to be careful not to go too deep into the subject. However, many of these topics lend themselves to having checklists or guides for execution. Blank OPORD and report shells, PCI checklists, priorities of work – the list goes on. Be cautious about over reliance or misuse of these materials during training and execution. Just as a helicopter pilot uses a preflight checklist to ensure all steps are done, she still must have thorough knowledge of the purpose and the "why" of the process. Learning the processes behind the lists and frameworks is the important component. The checklists we use are only a tool to remind and keep us on track when we are cold, wet, hungry, and out of our minds tired.

Citizens in our units must be the good guys in this mess; leaders must continually reinforce this fact with their fighters. Being violent and lethal without governance and morals will quickly devolve into wanton criminal opportunism. Leaders are managers of this violence and must ensure their unit maintains the moral high ground as they cycle in and out of lethal acts against a potentially less than moral enemy. Executing prisoners, theft of supplies from the local population (friendly or neutral), randomly searching homes and treating neutrals poorly is a great way to build opponents to your cause. We fully acknowledge this is easy to say this during normal times. It can be challenged as extremely naïve to have this view absent the backdrop of extreme personal suffering and loss, but the negative strategic implications of rage driven revenge killing of a surrendering enemy are well known and must be restrained.

Squad Organization

Looking at this through a realistic pre-event lens, we know that the opportunity for *most* groups to train at greater than squad or small platoon numbers is rare. This does not mean we can't take the opportunity to train at these levels, but as we discussed in the introduction our time in this manual is best spent learning and training for the typical group. At the outset of X Hour small unit actions will be more likely for an irregular force but will grow to company and even battalion size (based on historical examples of foreign occupation or invasion). This is an unknown, however what we do know is having tactically proficient squad/platoon and smaller elements will be the foundation to build these larger organizations as a conflict progresses.

18

Real Talk

Those in the prepper and minuteman community talk a lot about teams and groups as the only way to survive. We wholeheartedly agree with the necessity of a cohesive community and group that works together during a crisis. Personnel will always be our greatest challenge, especially prior to the X hour event when the perception of "normal" is high. Finding fellow humans who are willing, trainable, and capable of these tasks is difficult. From the pool of the willing only a few will truly commit. Of those that commit only a few of these individuals will be capable. Of the willing and capable odds are there will be a percentage that will hesitate or be a no show when a real crisis presents itself. The reality is you may have to do much of the initial prep work and training with very few teammates while you build or find your larger team. Until an event severe enough to be the forcing function for people to come together you may find it difficult to influence others to participate in training and preparation. Training alone is not optimal by any stretch of the imagination, but don't feel shame or "less than" if you are doing a lot of this on your own or with very few teammates (at least initially). Yes, it should absolutely be a top priority to find a fire team, then a squad/group but please don't paralyze yourself with inaction waiting to find others of the same mindset. This is not to be confused with the lone wolf mentality that we warned against, low numbers are simply part of reality for many of us.

Organizing for Combat

The organization and billets (the assignment, capabilities, and role aligned to a particular position) inside your group are just a small piece of the problem set. The starting point is identifying your mission requirements then building your organizational structure to meet those requirements and the anticipated mission profile outlined in CM-1. These include the unconventional/guerilla versions discussed

19

earlier: conducting recon operations, property or neighborhood security patrols, limited attacks in the form of ambushes, sabotage, and limited raids in support of a larger conventional force. The following organizational structures are just one way (aka "A" way) of allocating resources against these missions. You can adjust and tailor organizational structure, roles, and responsibilities to meet *your* requirements; you know your METT-TC factors better than anyone else. Improvise and adapt this material to fit your needs; you can use and vary the information in the manual as a guide to build out your SOPs.

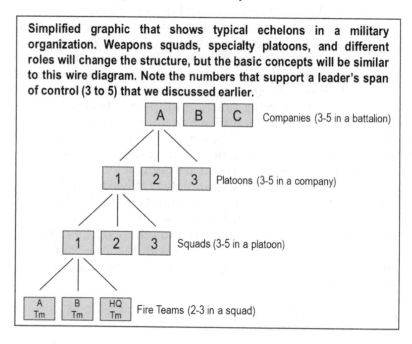

Simplified graphic that shows typical echelons in a military organization. Weapons squads, specialty platoons, and different roles will change the structure, but the basic concepts will be similar to this wire diagram. Note the numbers that support a leader's span of control (3 to 5) that we discussed earlier.

A   B   C   Companies (3-5 in a battalion)

1   2   3   Platoons (3-5 in a company)

1   2   3   Squads (3-5 in a platoon)

A Tm   B Tm   HQ Tm   Fire Teams (2-3 in a squad)

The roles and responsibilities we will lay out are not absolute (in most cases). You will use these to apply the capabilities to your situation. Yes, it is exponentially better to have a full team, but we must be honest with ourselves. There will be use cases for some in our preparedness community who will be required to conduct one man property patrols. This will especially be the case in the early stages of an event while things take shape and people hang on to a reality that no longer exists. The key is to do some critical thinking and apply the concepts and organizational structure in this manual to your set of circumstances and resources - even if you are solo.

Terms in this Section

Patrol. It is not a prescriptive term with regards to a specific mission task (eg we don't patrol as *the* mission), it refers to a unit that is planning, preparing, or executing the patrol. Patrols are sent out to conduct a specific combat, reconnaissance, or security mission. A patrol's organization is temporary and specifically matched to the immediate task but may be conducted by you as your organic unit (organic is the way you are typically organized without external assets attached).

Squad. A small unit of fighters organized into two or three fire teams. Each member has specified and implied responsibilities and operates under a single leader (the squad leader (SL)) with subordinate leaders (TLs) leading the fire teams. There can be two or three fire teams comprising a squad of 7 individuals up to a max of 12 to 13.

LD. Line of Departure is a graphic control measure designated to coordinate the departure of attack elements. When we say we are going to LD it is the true stepping off point for a mission; there may be tactical movement before LD but this is where things get real as units cross into threat territory and begin coordinating actions. It is treated as a verb as well, as in "we LD at 0330 tomorrow".

Patrol Leader. Exactly as it sounds, he or she leads the patrol. They can be a platoon leader, squad leader, fire team leader of none of these. If he is in charge of the unit conducting the patrol, he is the patrol leader and is responsible for everything the patrol does or fails to do. His duties and responsibilities are aligned to a particular mission; there are no administrative / garrison type duties that a patrol leader is aligned with other than those conducted during mission prep and TLPs. It is not a permanent organizational position in the group, those are the platoon, squad, or fire team leaders. If an organic unit is conducting a patrol the unit leader is the patrol leader by default. As groups develop always keep in mind that training, equipping, and developing leaders is the true challenge you will have to tackle.

"A" Way. Term used to provide examples that can be used in total or in part to help standardize organizational or tactical requirements. Descriptive in nature, it does not imply that this is *the* way, just a starting point that you can use for further development, adjustment, and application for your requirements.

Only a belt fed can be a belt fed. Unless you have machine guns in your formations you must find a way to fill the capability gap in your squad.

Light Support Weapon (LSW). We must be creative to bridge the capability gap of not having belt fed machine guns in our teams (unless belt fed weapons are available in your group). We cannot replicate these assets, *only a belt fed can be a belt fed*. But you can add weapon variants from the open market to boost the capability of your squad. Pseudo-doctrinally an LSW is akin to what a SAW brought to a formation - but in a semi-auto form. For our purposes a Light Support Weapon is a 5.56 or 7.62x39 magazine fed rifle (match the caliber to your team carbines), usually with a drum magazine. It will have a heavier profile 14.5-20 inch barrel able to withstand a *slightly* increased rapid and sustained firing rate. The firing rate (even with the heavier barrel) is limited and not sustainable like an MG but will still be better than a government or pencil profile barrel. It will have a magnified optic of some type, may have a lightweight bipod, and can provide enhanced suppressive fire capability at max effective range of the chosen round.

Your LSW gunners may (and should) provide you with a DMR-like capability as well to squeeze as much out of a single system as possible. It is not a belt fed nor does it serve in an automatic rifleman role. This is NOT the intent of having this role and weapon setup; the LSW in your formation is simply *slightly* more capable of providing suppression through precision or volume (very limited volume) versus the typical carbine in your squad.

The LSW is a more capable carbine that you may already own. It can be rifle or carbine, but should be heavy barreled to withstand a slightly higher rate of fire. It should also fit into that DMR role as well, everything has to do double duty in an unsupported force.

Heavy Support Weapon (HSW). A heavy support weapon / heavy machine gun is traditionally something in the .50 caliber or 12.7mm category. However, our categorization of an HSW for the Pro Citizen is akin to the terminal ballistic capabilities of a General Purpose Machine Gun (GPMG). The HSW in our formations is a .308 (or comparable) magazine fed rifle, capable of being fitted with a drum magazine, a magnified optic, and has a lightweight bipod. The HSW provides an enhanced suppressive capability (by precision, extended range, and/or somewhat increased volume) at max effective range of the chosen round; typically around 1,000 meters for this cartridge. It is not a machine gun nor does it pretend to serve in the machine gun / GPMG role. We aren't fooling ourselves; we are simply referring to it as HSW to differentiate it from the LSW. You can call it whatever you like, the intent here is to differentiate the capabilities so we can plan and train for them in our formations. The HSW (as defined here) can be added as a very capable system to enhance the squad's firepower through the addition of a larger caliber and a bit more capable round.

The HSW is a 7.62x51 (.308) magazine fed rifle. It provides additional suppression (and potentially DMR) capability for the squad. It is not a machine gun, so don't plan to use it in the same manner as a belt fed.

The Nine Man Squad ("A" way)

Squad Leader (SL)

A Tm Leader (TL)   RM   HSW Gunner   RM   B Tm Leader (TL)   RM   HSW Gunner   USO

LEGEND:
RM: Rifleman
SL: Squad leader
TL: Team Leader
LSW: Light Support Weapon (5.56 or 7.62x39)
HSW: Heavy Support Weapon (7.62x51 or 7.62x54R)
USO: Unmanned Sensor Operator
RTO: Radio Telephone Operator

Heavy Squad ("A" way)

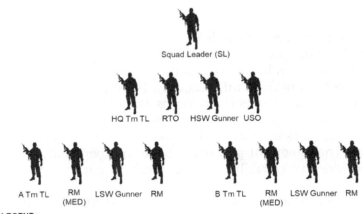

Squad Leader (SL)

HQ Tm TL   RTO   HSW Gunner   USO

A Tm TL   RM (MED)   LSW Gunner   RM   B Tm TL   RM (MED)   LSW Gunner   RM

LEGEND:
RM: Rifleman
SL: Squad leader
TL: Team Leader
LSW: Light Support Weapon (5.56 or 7.62x39)
HSW: Heavy Support Weapon (7.62x51 or 7.62x54R)
USO: Unmanned Sensor Operator
RTO: Radio Telephone Operator
MED: Medic, Combat Lifesaver, EMT etc

25

Roles and Responsibilities

Roles and Responsibilities for our organizations are greatly expanded and may not align with military doctrine. To fill the gaps by not having a robust military-like structure we must re-align tasks and build our organizations in a different way. ***Leadership in an irregular force will perform duties normally done by leaders two (or even three) levels higher than usual.*** For example, a squad leader operating as an independent patrol must be company commander, platoon leader, and squad leader all rolled into one. We will focus on actual mission execution responsibilities in this manual, the leader/positional responsibilities during pre-event training and admin tasks are not in the scope of our discussion here. This is just a guide; adapt and adjust these to suit your specific circumstances. The important part to understand is when no one is assigned a particular responsibility, the task will most likely not be accomplished. Tasks require assignment, an individual is aligned and held responsible for everything we do.

The roles and responsibilities outlined here are "A" way. The learning point is you must deliberately align patrol responsibilities by ability, not by duty position (while taking the workload into account). For example, your USO (Unmanned Systems Operator) is ideally your Intel expert, however he may not have that skillset. This role may be filled by a rifleman from a fire team, and that is perfectly fine. The important part is you have an expert that provides that capability in your group or unit.

Task Saturation. Task overload is a constant issue, we must ensure we aren't loading our most talented fighters down with more work than they can do effectively (this includes yourself and your subordinate leaders). Task Saturation is when one has too much to do without the mental capacity or time to execute it; a fighter's brain will essentially "lock up" when overloaded. Be careful about

26

giving your strongest team members too much to do, it is human nature to over-task the high performers.

Mission Essential Task. If everything is a priority, then nothing is a priority. We do not have the resources or time to maintain proficiency in every task. This concept dips into the training management realm a bit, but it is something we recommend considering at this point in your progress. Mission Essential Tasks (MET) are well-defined tasks that must be executed to accomplish the next higher unit's warfighting mission (the concept of nesting tasks was introduced in CM-1). Everything is nested or is supported by tasks at lower echelons of units all the way down to individuals. For example, you determine it is mission essential for your group/unit to be proficient at conducting an area reconnaissance. A supporting collective task (SCT) might be *occupy an Objective Rally Point (ORP).* Some of the associated individual tasks that support this nested task might be *navigate by dead reckoning at night, send a SPOTREP,* and even something that seems tangential such as *apply a tourniquet to a casualty.* This is just to name a few; the list of tasks is extensive.

These individual tasks are associated with standards as well, during training we can't just tell our team members to "go do navigation" without an achievable, measurable result (a standard) that also supports the larger collective task (the ORP occupation in our area recon example). This manual does not specify these full tasks, conditions, and standards that comprise a legitimately developed task as we want to keep this section manageable for this document. This is why we are capturing these in a non-doctrinal manner as "Mission Essential Skills" (not "tasks"). We list some of these with each squad position in the organization section so you can form your approach to developing and training your team members.

27

Mission Essential Skills are progressive. For example, the Squad Leader must be proficient in all the common essential skills, the team leader skills, as well as the squad leader skills. ***The following skills for each position are far from an exhaustive list; they are presented to generate thought and provide a framework for you to expand for your training.*** You can use these to develop your own detailed set of tasks and standards for your anticipated mission set using these general guidelines.

Every Citizen in a Patrol

Responsibilities *(applies to everyone in the team including all leaders).* In general, a patrol member is responsible for:

Responsibilities All Patrol Members	
	• entering the mission at a high level of physical fitness.
	• safe weapons handling and having a well maintained and zeroed long gun with recorded holdovers.
	• always knowing where they are on the map.
	• understanding the unit SOP and all battle drills.
	• performing basic lifesaving medical tasks.
	• maintaining noise, light, litter, and signal discipline during patrols and remaining alert during movement and at halts.
	• articulating the commander's intent (the "why" or intended effects) for the mission; taking the initiative during patrols to fill in gaps left by personnel shortages.
	• being physically, mentally, and tactically proficient to take charge of a unit two levels up (eg a Fire Team leader must be ready to step up and lead a platoon).

Mission Essential Skills for every member of the patrol *(not an exhaustive list)*:

• hit a stationary IPSC size target during daylight with their rifle/carbine (in any zone, units must set specific zone standards and percentages) at distances from zero to 400 meters

• hit a stationary IPSC size target (in any zone, units can set specific zone standards and percentages) with their rifle/carbine at PID distance (dependent on weather and light conditions) using **passive** night vision

• run three miles in PT (Physical Training) gear (typical running attire) on relatively flat terrain in under 24 minutes

• enter and clear a room, hallway, stairwell as a member of a team (will be addressed in future manuals)

• execute individual movement techniques and move tactically as a member of a formation

• ruck 12 miles on a cleared trail/road in three hours or less with your group's baseline summer/warm weather Approach Load (it is ok to not use weapons for measuring this if you are training in a non-permissive or public space, just account for the weight in another way)

• stop massive bleeding, conduct CPR, and treat for shock (apply MARCH casualty treatment priorities)

• move and maneuver at night with and without NV systems

• accurately navigate to a point on the ground using dead reckoning, terrain association, and GPS systems

The Patrol Leader / Squad Leader (SL)

The squad leader is typically the most experienced member of the squad (we will address leadership attributes and leader development in detail inside other CM manuals). He or she will be the patrol leader for missions that are assigned to or are self-directed for the squad. Remember a patrol leader can be at any echelon at company and below. We are focusing on the SL as the patrol leader in this section, but it can be any individual leading a patrol. SL roles and responsibilities for the Citizen organization are expanded significantly compared to a SL in an organized force. In this irregular organization they must be capable of operating autonomously and remotely for extended periods of time. He must understand how to integrate his squad into a larger force or operate in support of local authorities. When operating independently he must shoulder platoon sergeant and platoon leader tasks as well as the typical SL duties and responsibilities. If you have a group larger than squad size these duties can be reallocated back up to the appropriate leader, but for our purposes we must assume that the squad size element is going to be the focus of the pre-event training effort.

The SL is responsible for what the squad does or fails to do. This includes tactical employment, training, personnel management, and logistics. This is done by planning, making timely decisions, issuing orders, assigning tasks, and supervising patrol activities. He knows his fighters and how and when to employ the patrol's weapons and electronic assets. The SL is responsible for positioning and employing all specialty weapons (Heavy support weapons, DMRs, snipers or the chance addition of belt fed guns) and employment of any special capabilities / combat multipliers such as drones, electronic surveillance etc. Some of the specific SL duties are listed below.

Responsibilities. In general, the SL is responsible for:

<table>
<tr>
<td rowspan="2" style="writing-mode: vertical-rl">**Responsibilities Squad Leader**</td>
<td>

• the well-being and safety of patrol members; not taking unnecessary risks with their lives.

• mission planning, time management, and issuing orders (WARNO, OPORD, FRAGO).

• keeping his higher HQ/command post (if present) informed by using periodic situation reports (SITREPs).

• employment of special weapons and sensors (purpose, location, and timing).

• requests more support for the patrol from higher HQ if needed to perform the mission.

• planning and coordinating the patrol's sustainment effort and casualty evacuation (CASEVAC) plan.

• ensuring all-around security (including air threats) is maintained.

• supervising and spot-check of all assigned tasks and corrects unsatisfactory actions.
</td>
</tr>
</table>

Mission Essential Skills for the SL (not an exhaustive list):

• conduct Troop Leading Procedures (including TLP in time constrained environments).

• write and orally issue clear, concise mission type orders in recognized standard formats to subordinates.

• plan routes and direct the appropriate formations and techniques of movement for the patrol.

31

• accurately report information to higher headquarters to include SITREPS, SPOTREPS and others as required.

• assign team and HSW priorities and sectors of fire.

• conduct detailed rehearsals and pre combat inspections to ensure team members understand mission, intent, and have fully mission capable gear and equipment.

• assign collection priorities and cueing (when to use) guidance to the USO (Unmanned Sensor Operator).

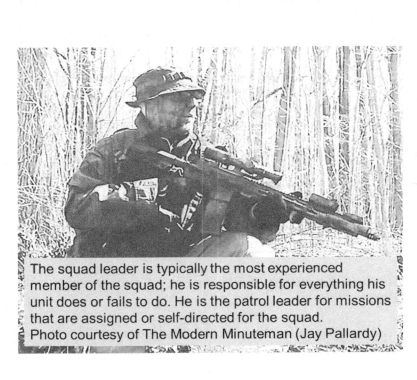

The squad leader is typically the most experienced member of the squad; he is responsible for everything his unit does or fails to do. He is the patrol leader for missions that are assigned or self-directed for the squad.
Photo courtesy of The Modern Minuteman (Jay Pallardy)

Headquarters Team Leader (HTL)

The HTL (this is non-doctrinal) in a heavy squad acts as an assistant patrol leader and performs many of what would be platoon sergeant duties. He leads the HQ Fire Team and assists the SL with special capabilities employment. To say the HTL will have their hands full is an understatement. They must be incredibly mature and be comfortable with delegating and supervising tasks. Adding an additional 10th individual in the 9 man squad model can provide you with a similar capability. In a traditional 9 man squad having an experienced RTO or USO fire team member who fills the assistant patrol leader role may be more effective than using the A or B Tm leaders to perform these PSG/HTL duties, just be cautious about task saturation. Keep in mind these concepts are "A" way, figure out what works for your unit as personalities and capabilities will drive your choice.

The HTL is the next senior in the patrol and second in succession of command. The HTL helps and advises the SL, leads the patrol in the leader's absence, supervises the patrol's administration, logistics, and maintenance, and prepares and issues Paragraph 4 of the operation order (OPORD).

If your heavy squad includes an HTL he is an incredible asset. He will take up the slack for platoon sergeant type patrol tasks to prevent SL task overload.

33

Responsibilities. In general the HTL is responsible for:

Responsibilities

Headquarters Team Leader

• organizing and controlling the patrol command post (CP) according to the unit SOP.

• supervising and directs the patrol medic(s) and patrol aid-litter teams in moving casualties to the rear.

• patrol status of personnel, weapons, and equipment to include the morale, discipline, and health of patrol members. Enforces field discipline and preventive medicine measures.

• supervising task-organized elements of the patrol including the security forces during withdrawals, support elements during raids or attacks and security patrols during night attacks (some of these tasks are aligned to missions outside the scope of this manual but we need to account for these skillsets so you can put the right team member in this position).

• coordinating and supervising patrol resupply operations and ensures that ammunition, supplies, and loads are properly and evenly distributed.

• assisting the SL in supervising and spot-checking all assigned tasks and correcting unsatisfactory actions.

• supervises security at the ORP (Objective Rally Point) and assists in patrol base (PB) occupation and adjusting the perimeter.

Mission Essential Skills for the HTL *(not an exhaustive list):*

• track and manage the unit's basic load (the supplies physically carried into the fight) prior to operations, monitor supply status during missions and plan resupply.

• direct the medics and aid/litter teams in moving casualties.

• establishes, marks, supervises the planned casualty collection point (CCP), and ensures that the personnel status including wounded in action (WIA) or killed in action (KIA) is accurately reported to your group's HQ.

• track the patrol's water status and develop the water plan (*this is critical*) during TLPs.

• ensure LSW and HSW sectors are set properly during patrol base occupation; validates sector sketches.

Team Leader (to include Scout Team Leaders)

The fire team leader (TL) is a fighting leader who leads by example. He is responsible for all his team does or fails to do, and is responsible for caring of the team's people, weapons, and equipment. He or she is the first level of direct leadership in a tactical unit, and as such the TL is a critical position for you to select. The Fire Team Leader is constantly balancing his responsibilities as a leader with his role as a member of a team that directly engages the enemy. The TL leads a fire team of 3 to 5 individuals in combat. Positional authority enables him to enforce discipline in the field and ensure his team members act as a cohesive unit. He accomplishes assigned missions using initiative without needing constant guidance from the SL or HTL.

The Fire Team Leader (TL) is the first level of direct leadership in a unit. They lead by example and always take the initiative to ensure their team is squared away.

Responsibilities. In general, the Team Leader is responsible for:

Responsibilities
Team Leader

• adjusting the team's formation based on the effectiveness of the enemy's fire and available cover and concealment.

• leading his team in fire and movement.

• controlling the movement of his team and its rate and distribution of fire.

• security of the team's area of operations.

• assisting the squad leader and HTL as required.

Mission Essential Skills for a TL (*not an exhaustive list*):

• maneuvering the team using individual movement techniques (IMT), buddy team fire and movement, and fire team fire and movement (maneuver).

• monitors the team's health, water, ammo and equipment status and inform the SL/HTL of any support requirements.

• spot check PCCs and tracks weapons and ammo status of the team

HSW or LSW Gunner

These are not belt fed / automatic rifleman roles. We cannot replace or replicate the capability of a belt fed M249 or M240B with a magazine fed gun. This is NOT the intent of having this role and weapon setup. The LSW or HSW is a bit more capable of providing suppression through precision or volume (albeit very limited) versus the standard / typical AR in the squad. Adding true belt-fed machineguns to a unit is always the better solution.

Responsibilities. In general, the LSW and HSW gunners are additionally responsible for:

Responsibilities LSW / HSW	
	• **providing accurate and high(er) volume of small arms fire for the squad.**
	• **assisting the SL or HTL with weapon emplacement.**

Mission Essential Skills for an LSW/HSW *(not an exhaustive list):*

• hit a standard IPSC size steel silhouette at 600 meters (LSW) 800 meters (HSW) during daylight (specific standards, hit percentages, and conditions are established by your unit).

• hit a standard IPSC size silhouette at PID distance during limited visibility.

• manage rates of fire in accordance with the weapon capability and ammo conservation requirements.

RTO / Assistant BICC

The RTO is a member of the HQ Team. He is an expert at operating and employing the squad's communication systems. The RTO communicates with the higher HQ (if present) for the patrol, sending all reports and information. He works closely with the patrol leader to manage communication requirements. He assists the BICC with information collection, recording, and reporting. He assists the SL with communications plans and writes Paragraph 5 (Command and Signal) of the OPORD for the SL's review. He is an expert at RF signal management, counter-intercept, and terrain signal masking.

Not your grandfather's RTO. Our RTOs are experts at comms, RF signal management, counter-intercept, power management, and terrain signal masking.

Responsibilities. In general the RTO is responsible for:

<table>
<tr>
<td rowspan="2">Responsibilities</td>
<td rowspan="2">RTO</td>
<td>

• **planning, establishing, and maintaining electronic communications within the team and to higher HQ.**

• **building the rehearsal site / terrain model for the squad.**

• **assist the USO with power and battery management plan for the HQ team and builds field-expedient antennas as needed.**

</td>
</tr>
</table>

Mission Essential Skills for an RTO (not an exhaustive list):

• manage the electronic signature of the squad's communications.

• manage the squad's communication plan to include frequency allocation, encryption, and codes.

• during mission analysis and IPB he assesses the threat electronic warfare capabilities and recommends appropriate countermeasures to the patrol leader.

USO / BICC

The Unmanned Sensor Operator (USO) is a member of the HQ Team. He is an expert at operating and employing the squad's unmanned systems. The USO should also be the battlefield information coordination center (BICC) for the patrol, compiling and recording all reports and information. He works closely with the patrol leader and the RTO to manage information requirements.

Responsibilities. In general the USO is responsible for:

Responsibilities USO	• assisting the SL (patrol leader) with information management.
	• planning and employing the unmanned systems for the patrol (most likely unmanned aerial systems / drones).
	• assisting the patrol leader as required during TLP and missions.

Mission Essential Skills for the USO *(not an exhaustive list):*

• plan unmanned system and sensor employment during TLPs in accordance with SL / patrol leader guidance.

• employ unmanned systems to confirm or deny information requirements in accordance with the OPORD.

• mitigate electronic signature while employing unmanned systems by using terrain masking and other passive countermeasures.

• maintain and repair the patrol's unmanned systems.

• manage the power consumption and battery management plan for the HQ team to include the patrol leader's and HTL's batteries.

• coordinate with the HTL and emplace tripwire and/or electronic early warning systems for patrol bases.

• understand and assist the patrol leader with the IPB process; record and manage intelligence reports for the patrol, collect and consolidate reports for submission.

Gear and Equipment

Mission drives the gear, but we may not have the luxury of multiple options when the crisis happens. Your gear and firearm choices must be in tune with your anticipated mission set to support legitimate, real-world requirements. These gear requirements are based on your research, lessons learned during training, personal and regional assessments (IPB), and wargaming. We will cover specific gear and equipment setup tips for the Scout a bit later in Chapter 2.

Fast and mobile. Carrying only the items you truly need while staying agile and quiet is what we are after. Do your homework to assess what you really need to carry - and then test that loadout under realistic conditions to assess the balance of speed and weight. photo courtesy of IG @RhodeIslandAboriginal

Load Definitions

Keeping loads manageable and preventing injury cannot be overemphasized. We need sustainable, tailorable, light(ish) loads that our fighters can carry. Loads that provide capability but are also light enough to preserve the speed and agility advantages of a guerilla force. We still must do this without freezing to death or having inadequate ammo for the mission; these are the ever-present series of tradeoffs. A lightly armed force must offset the lack of firepower with agility, speed, and stealth. Weighing an individual down with gear detracts from those advantages, our challenge is always this balancing act of capability vs weight and the resulting effect on speed.

Always keep this speed detriment in mind as you work on loadouts and balance your requirements with the mobility advantage that a guerilla force needs.

Fighting Load consists of the equipment and clothing (including your pocket contents) that is worn or carried directly on a fighter while maneuvering and fighting. As a *general guideline*, the weight of a fighting load should not exceed one-third of your body weight. This is known as the "33% rule". The weight of a fighting load piles up quickly as it is anything you have on your body - to include boots, uniform, pocket contents, chest rig etc. By doctrine a fighting load is only what you carry once contact has been made with the enemy and consists of the essential items needed to accomplish your task during the engagement. We highly recommend expanding that to include adequate water and shelter to keep yourself going for 24 hours (cold weather will change this approach a bit as there is a limit to how much we should carry in a Fighting Load). The backpacking community likes to measure loads as "base weight" to account for the constantly carried items vs consumables. While this can be a useful approach it will not give you an accurate read on the true weight you and your team will be carrying. Since we will never start off with empty mags, dry canteens, or vacant food bags we should account for consumables (ammo, water, nutrition etc) when measuring your total weights.

Everybody feeds the pig. Everyone will be carrying additional ammo for the HSW (or belt fed if they are available). Plan for this during team training and TLPs. You don't want a team member surprised that he must carry a D50 drum mag or an MG belt in his pack as well as his own ammo.

We must have contingencies for when we are separated from our rucks or primary sustainment packs with all our "stuff". Our 24 hour recommendation goes along with this thought. It is inevitable you will get separated from your ruck at some point. The other inevitability is when you do get separated from it the weather or conditions will shift from blue sky beautiful to rain and 42 degrees. Or the two hour OP becomes two days due to changes in the situation. We must tailor and manage our fighting loads to ensure we account for this eventuality. The Fighting Load Matrix on the following page is simply an example of something you can use to start to plan your loads and account for weight, it is not an encompassing list. Items, methods of carrying, and quantities are all things you need to assess through the lens of your actual requirements and your local unit SOPs. You may carry a small amount of Class I (food/nutrition) with you on your fighting load, additional specialized equipment, or seasonal clothing or protection that are not listed. If you see them as necessary for your requirements, then add them to your version of the matrix. *Water will be a larger issue than many consider*, carrying water and redundant means of processing non-potable water is beyond critical.

The use of body armor (hard plate) is always an option, we must be smart about when and where we decide to wear it. The same goes for ballistic helmets (other than during night for NV). Contrary to popular military sentiment, Protection is not always synonymous with Survivability. Being able to move fast and quiet can oftentimes holistically boost survivability more than a ballistic helmet and SAPI plates. There are few absolutes in this business, and as we always say, adjust this information to fit your requirements. Keep in mind this and other manuals in the Professional Citizen Project are not focused on endless roaming of the wastelands in the post-apocalyptic world. This is built around realistic missions of property patrols, local reconnaissance, and surveillance. Missions lasting anywhere from a few minutes to two or three days...but will repeat over and over against the backdrop of a crisis that has no end in sight. This is a marathon, not a sprint so set your kit up (and your mindset) to support the long haul.

Baseline Fighting Load Minimum Reqirements Example (adjust to meet your mission requirements)

Fighting Loads for USO, HSW etc will be adjusted to support their tasks

Water	5 quarts minimum recommended	Carrying methods per SOP, environment, and personal preference
Water treatment / water filter	Indiviudual water filter and/or water treatment chemicals	Type per personal preference, unit SOP, and your environment
Seasonal Uniform	Camo pattern long sleeve and long pants Head Cover (Cravat, Patrol Cap (PC), or boonie)	directed by team SOP
Primary Weapon with loaded mag	Minimum of four (4) primary weapon mags on load carriage rig (for a total of 5 *minimum*; **METT-TC will drive this number for you**)	
Load Carriage	Can be LBE, Chest Rig, LBV, Plate Carrier or combination to support your requirements	May include an assault pack
IFAK	(1) Tourniquet (CAT or SOF-T) (primary TQs should be carried on gear or on person and be covered) (1) Emergency Trauma /Israeli Dressing - 4" (1) Chest Seal (Vented) (2) Wound Packing Gauze (2) Gloves (not black, blood will not show well on black gloves during blood sweeps) (1) Duct Tape-Mini - 2" X 100" (1) Casualty Card	This is a baseline or minimum list, addition of other items is encouraged. Airways and decompression needles (if trained) etc are always great to have on hand.
Fixed Blade Knife	High quality full-tang fixed blade	Can be a sharpened bayonet as long as it can also serve as a field knife
Light Amplification NV system	PVS14 or dual tube NV	Batteries in quantity to support the mission
Mounting platform for NV	Helmet, head harness etc	Recommended that if you choose helmet it is a ballistic version
Red Lens Light	Handheld, micro light, headlamp	Use caution when using per light discipline concepts
Lighter	Recommend carrying two	
Camo face paint	Colors to match your environment	
Waterproof notebook with pencil and pen		
Compass	Lensatic (primary) and a backup (baseplate)	
Map	Waterproofing or map case	
Coordinate scale (protractor)	MapTools brand coordinate scale or mil issue GTA	Ensure your scale is correct for your map
GPS	Wrist mounted or handheld; account for batteries for mission duration	Have well-defined SOPs for these, be judicious with their use as tracklogs from a captured GPS unit are
Secondary Firearm (if used) with magazines	Carrying a secondary is driven by METT-TC	
Map markers	permanent (waterproof) with method to erase	
Signaling Devices	Whistle, VS17 panel, chem light, IR strobe etc	Per your unit SOP
Radio	Account for batteries in your loadouts	radios may be for leaders only per your SOP
Binos / magnified monocular	8x waterporoof binos, 8x monocular	Shared / as required by your SOP
Thermal Sight / Sensor	May be shared across the team	Shared / as required by your SOP

45

Approach Load consists of the fighting load plus a rucksack or main pack carried during a march or movement, which would contain additional water, ammunition, food, and other supplies for the duration of the mission. An approach load contains the essential equipment carried in addition to the fighting load. These items are dropped in an assault position, Objective Rally Point (ORP), or other spot before or upon contact with the enemy. For extended operations we must carry enough equipment and munitions to fight and exist until the mission is completed or a planned resupply can take place. The approach load and fighting load will morph and blend together by mission. Assault packs may be considered part of the Fighting Load or Approach Load vs carrying the full rucksack. The learning point is there must be a balance struck between items carried benefit vs the negative impact of the weight. The Approach Load should remain under 40% of total body weight.

Patrolling is not rucking. Keeping loads manageable but capable will help prevent injury and maintain the speed advantage of the guerilla force. It isn't about how much you can "man up" and carry, it is about mission analysis and tailoring loads to fit the task and purpose.

Be conscious of the fact that you may carry the approach load almost the entire time during some reconnaissance missions. There will be little to no resupply, so plan accordingly. Excessive approach loads must be configured so the additional weight can be redistributed or shed (leaving only the fighting load) before or upon contact with the enemy. There is no way to predict this with 100 percent accuracy, but the more analysis and training we do prior to a mission the more tailored our loads will become. Thinking through this process we understand the patrol may be surviving from a fighting load for more time than originally intended. If you are being deliberately and relentlessly pursued by the enemy after direct fire contact you will most likely drop (and optimally destroy) your approach load. You aren't going to IMT with a full ruck, you will drop it when direct fire contact is made. With these unpredictable situations just know that once you are separated from your main ruck (be it deliberate or not) you may never see it again. The learning point is there may be circumstances when you will operate with less than you had planned on.

Digging tools. A small shovel or Entrenching Tool (E Tool) is a necessity. Carrying E Tools had fallen out of favor for a couple of decades, but they are solidly in the required column of most mission loadout lists. There is a weight penalty to carry them, but concealment, fighting positions, and sanitation during missions are requirements we must consider.

Drills, contingency plans, and training scenarios for your team should account for this possibility.

Emergency Approach March Load. Circumstances could require us to carry excess loads (greater than 45 percent of body weight) such as approach marches through terrain impassable by vehicles or when ground transportation resources are not available or tactically sound. Do not make this your default as the bearer (that is you by the way) will quickly become fatigued and possibly injured.

Loadout Weight. Heavy loads can have the reverse of the intended effect by *reducing* combat effectiveness. It is a balancing act of what you need for the mission versus the physical detriment of that load. We know through common sense and experience that slower movement under contact will result in a much higher probability of being hit. The lighter you are, the faster you will be and the less likely you will be hit.

Gear layers and planned priorities. You probably remember during the GWOT days a popular approach was gear lines. "First line" did this, "Second Line" did that etc. Some still use it as an approach which is fine, just realize that way of thinking was for a supported force and optimized for a different kind of fight. The Fighting Load and Approach Load doctrine also leaves a lot of gray area for us as well. I would submit we have to approach the problem by combining these ideas together and apply reality. We must account for being separated from or being required to abandon gear *during* a mission. A fighting load in 40 degrees and rain had better account for some of those shelter items that were usually associated with Third Line or Approach Load using those concepts. You may have components of shelter split between your 24 hour Fighting Load and your Approach load (main ruck). Wargame it through the lens of what you will take off first and when. What will you still have on you? What are my capabilities after I shed that part of my kit? And more importantly can I fight and survive with what is left after each iteration of the process?

48

This isn't a gear abandonment exercise where we randomly dump a piece of kit when it becomes inconvenient to carry. This is the reality of being a Scout. Leaving your ruck in an ORP to go recon an objective ... and then getting cut off from the ORP. Or the ORP gets overrun, and your security element has to displace. Are you going to conduct a four-man assault to recover your poncho from your ruck? Of course not, so Chicom Charlie gets to eat your MREs and stay dry with your poncho tonight. Do you have enough items on your LBE to continue the mission...or even survive? Anytime you put your ruck down (referred to as grounding) plan for contingency items in case you never see it again. It may be the example we used before; you are being relentlessly pursued by a determined enemy. As a Scout the potential for this is very real, lightening your load to put distance between you having to and the pursuing force.

Have contingencies in case you get separated from your gear. Inducing gear loss *("ok fellas, ground your rucks and leave them here for tonight")* during a team training weekend will be a significant emotional event for some.
Photo courtesy of The Modern Minuteman (Jay Pallardy)

Chapter 2
Scouting

This is where the basic individual tactical and movement skills you have learned from CM-1 start to come together and really level-up. Each patrol member must be knowledgeable in the principles of scouting. The squad organization and skills in Chapter 1 is only the starting point. Because of the anticipated mission set that will be recon and security heavy we recommend everyone in your organization become proficient at scouting. Before we discuss recon mission planning, unit movements, and battle drills we need to focus on the details of some related individual skills for those missions and concepts. A good Scout is a combination of expert woodsman, hunter, predator, ninja, and commando. Day or night and in all weather conditions a Scout must be able to move quietly and unobserved. Our imperative is always to see and not be seen (or go unnoticed in plain sight). The squad organizations in the prior chapter can be organized into smaller scout teams depending on your mission.

Five man, three man, even two man scout teams can be task organized and sent on coordinated recon missions to gather information for the squad or the higher headquarters. No matter what size organization you operate in there are common scout skills and knowledge that you will use. Any members from the squad may be called upon to conduct recon tasks, whether they are an HSW gunner or RTO they must be able to scout as we cannot afford to have a dedicated "one trick pony" in our formations.

The Scout

Some of these scout attributes listed below may appear redundant with the Professional Citizen basic individual and leader skills addressed in both the CM-1 and this manual. A Scout (capitalized to make it stand out a bit) must have more than baseline proficiency of these skills, he or she must be an absolute expert. The risk of being compromised, getting lost, or providing inaccurate enemy locations is far too great to employ untrained scouts. Scouts must be critical thinkers, able to assess situations rapidly and think several steps ahead. Make no mistake, it takes years of training and experience to be proficient at scouting and reconnaissance. Incorporating these concepts in your training consistently and developing the attributes will go a long way to building your skillset as you grow.

The Scout is skilled at camouflage and uses terrain to their advantage. He is an expert at moving quietly and remaining undetected for days at a time without external support.
Photo courtesy of The Modern Minuteman (Jay Pallardy)

Key attributes of a Scout

❒ They have well-developed Situational Awareness (SA); a Scout pays attention to detail and has a keen sense of pattern recognition. If something is slightly out of place, he will pick up on it.

❒ He is comfortable with mission type orders and operating in relative isolation without constant guidance (or support).

❒ The Scout is a critical thinker with a well-developed "terrain sense." They can visualize and predict the relationship between the terrain, friendly, and enemy forces.

❒ Scouts are expert map readers and navigators; they pride themselves on always knowing where they are and accurately plotting objects on the map.

❒ The Scout must be skilled at camouflage and using terrain to mask movement. They understand how to plan routes to recon objectives and always use the terrain to their advantage.

❒ He or she is an expert at moving silently through the terrain and is proficient at fieldcraft making him capable of remaining undetected while operating for days at a time without external support.

Terms for this section

Terrain sense. The ability to visualize and read terrain; it is an intangible skill that allows the leader or scout to "see" the terrain and how it will interact with humans and equipment. This is the mark of a great tactical leader.

Compromised. To be discovered or "busted" when scouting. An individual, team, position, or mission can be compromised. One quick point on this, the senior scout on the ground must have the authority to call missions off for *any* reason and self-extract or request extraction (if available).

Fieldcraft. The skills required to operate in the field such as stealth, camouflage, observation, shelter, water processing, and even hygiene/sanitation. These are the collection of skills that encompass "life out in the field" away from modern facilities. Fieldcraft is the set of skills needed to operate and survive with what is in your kit. These skills will be different across terrain types such as the eastern woodlands, southern swamps, northern tundra or western deserts and mountains. The Citizen will have limited or no external support at times. He or she will have to get by with what they have through creativity in using available resources while remaining undetected. Fieldcraft as a Scout is not camping, bushcrafting, or backpacking; fieldcraft has elements of all these but is the extension and holistic enhancement of your tactical survival skills.

Dead Space. An area within the maximum range of a weapon, sensor, or observer which cannot be covered by fire or observation from a particular position because of intervening obstacles, the nature of the ground, or the characteristics of the chosen weapon. The IV lines (intervisibility lines) discussed in CM-1 land nav section are a great example of dead space that may not be readily apparent to an observer.

Scout Camouflage and Remaining Unseen/Unnoticed

Nothing rattles, nothing shines. The Scout must be uncompromising in the techniques of stealth, deception, and avoidance of detection. This is the core of becoming an effective reconnaissance professional. The following section captures the building blocks and concepts you must master to be a great Scout. These apply day and night and in all weather conditions. Blend in and become part of the environment. This may include urban, suburban, desert, forest...the list goes on. The imperative is to disappear into your surroundings. Sometimes that means disappearing in plain sight; being seen but not noticed by wearing blue jeans and a work shirt with your CCW pistol (or even unarmed based on current risk). Sometimes it calls for a camouflaged uniform and face paint. It can be anything in between, you are only limited by your imagination and creative thinking.

Sometimes camo uniforms and tactical gear are inappropriate for scouting. The goal is to not be seen, or simply not be noticed while hiding in plain sight. Match local clothing choices to blend in or be creative to gain access to areas.

Weather, lighting conditions, and seasons all influence camouflage choice and techniques. When choosing your methods also account for persistent surveillance and electronic sensors that can detect outside of the visible spectrum; you must manage your camo scheme for sound and smells as well.

Indicators of presence. These are things we look for during our SLLS halts and observation techniques. They include *Movement, Noise, Shape and Outline, Color and Texture, Shine, Shadow, and Scent.* **Movement** and **Noise** are far and away the greatest giveaways, we will discuss them first. You may get lucky and be able to get away with some camo deficiencies or gear color mistakes, but movement and noise will compromise a Scout every time.

Movement. Any movement, especially fast, irregular, or furtive movement is the primary way to attract attention. It is what we look for in our ancient brains; movement indicates either danger or prey. By moving slowly and deliberately you decrease the chance of detection or compromise. Movement combined with a background that allows it to stand out is a real killer. When moving past obstacles such as fences avoid going over them, if you must go over keep your body level with the top of the fence or wall to avoid silhouetting. Do not silhouette yourself against the skyline when crossing hills or ridges. When moving, you will also have difficulty detecting the movement of a threat. Stop frequently, listen, and look around slowly (SLLS) to detect signs of hostile movement. It takes years to become proficient at putting all the patrolling skills together, but you can practice moving quietly anytime to hone this skill. This part seems like common sense - but stay out of open areas. It may be unavoidable for the terrain you are in (desert, plains etc), but if at all possible, avoid moving in the open if you are trying to remain unseen.

Noise. Noise attracts attention, especially if there is a sequence of loud noises such as several snapping branches. Rhythmic sounds indicate human presence so move in broken patterns when patrolling. Study how woodland mammals walk, they are alert and constantly observing their environment. A few steps, brief pauses to look and listen (almost a series of mini/micro SLLS halts is a good way to think about it). Do not plod along at a steady ruck march pace, vary your steps and these brief stops. We are patrolling, not just walking or ruck marching. Slow down your pace as much as necessary to avoid making excessive noise. Rolling your feet heel to toe, picking up your feet, watching foot placement to not break branches or dislodge rocks, and keeping shock-absorber spring in your strides. Doing this is exhausting, but necessary. It is inevitable that we will make some noise while moving through the terrain, don't be overly cautious to the point that it slows movement to ineffective rates. The point is we must be diligent to minimize noise, but there is no way to eliminate it completely during the entirety of a mission. During patrols you will not talk above a whisper, most times not talking at all. Hand and arm signals are the primary means of communication in a team.

When you use radio comms the speaker / mics must be turned down or off. Earpieces or headsets for monitoring are a great option since even the lowest volume radio mic speaker may be detectable by a nearby enemy. Sending reports over the radio is done at a whisper. Command posts need to get this in their heads as they listen to and take reports, and teams in the field must practice it. Normal voice volume comms for radio or audible commands are reserved for during direct fire contact only. Electronic devices must be silenced; shut off audible feedback on digital watches, GPS, and radio keypads.

Weapons need special attention for noise abatement. Sling attachment points, slings, covers etc all need silencing and pass a rattle check (see CM-1 for more details). Weapons maintenance in the field is time consuming, you must learn to keep basic weapons maintenance activities scentless and quiet. Unloading and loading silently for maintenance is a skillset that must be practiced. Releasing an M4 bolt carrier group to chamber a round is incredibly loud in the quiet woods or desert. You can train this at home with dummy rounds (no live ammo present); unload, clean, and then reload your carbine by quietly riding the charging handle forward to strip a new round off the mag and then use the forward assist to complete chambering.

During missions you can use background noises to cover your movement. The sounds of aircraft, trucks, generators, wind, and people talking will cover some or all the sounds produced by your movement. Rain will mask movement noise, but it also reduces our ability to detect enemy movement. If it covers our sound, it can also mask the threat.

Shape and Outline. When camouflaging yourself to disrupt outline consider that certain shapes are particular to humans or signs of human presence. Straight lines are rare in nature, as are the outlines of helmets or a ruck. Breaking up your outline by using scrim (a small covering such as a piece of a camo net attached to kit) is a technique, but we recommend being judicious in its use. Oftentimes the additional movement of the camo material itself and noise penalty of using excessive scrim is not worth it. Trial and error for your AO during training will reveal what works for you. Placing vegetation from the surroundings on yourself is a technique, but this is often not the best solution. Vegetation will wilt over time, and it can also accentuate movement through the woods. Displacing from one area to another, even over a short distance, may put you in an area where your chosen veggie camo is out of place (eg a clump of green ferns in an amber wheat field as an extreme illustrative example).

Color and Texture. Colors in the natural and man-made environments can be deceiving. To hide and conceal presence in any environment you must imitate the color and texture of your surroundings. Use man-made materials as the base of your camouflage and utilize camouflage paint schemes on long guns and equipment. Paint your defensive long gun(s) you will use in the field. If you are serious about this business the perceived "loss of resale value" should never be a factor for your defensive long gun.

Don't drive yourself crazy with being too specific on camo clothing choice, there is no perfect solution - so don't look for one. What may work in a clump of bushes you are currently in may not work after you walk a few yards. The requirement is to find a pattern and color that works for you in your AO most of the time. Unless you live in the desert southwest odds are you will have two (or even three) sets of patterns as the seasons change. Beware of your own pre-conceived notions and bias; a color and pattern you *know* to be the best can actually present issues when exposed to lighting changes. Do some research on current camouflage tests and demonstrations, there is plenty of good video content available that shows what patterns may have issues and what work well (to include performance under NV).

Texture defines the surface characteristics of an object and may be smooth, rough, rocky, leafy, or many other possible combinations. Using color and texture together is a best practice, further disrupting man-made objects with natural colored texture is the key. We don't need to look like moving trees, but there are small, efficient ways to add texture to items that have textures that are out of place in nature. Experiment and try different techniques and materials, but always prioritize usability and function in the process. Prevent the creation of a human snag hazard or weapon malfunctions induced by a loose piece of scrim.

Cover all areas of exposed skin, including face, hands, neck (including the back of your neck), and ears. The hands lead and have a lot of movement, yet camouflage is often neglected. Use camouflage paint or gloves when in the field. Gloves are the optimal solution as they provide protection as well. Getting used to wearing them even in hot, humid conditions will take some time but the protection is worth it since even a small injury can create a large issue in the field.

Use camouflage makeup on your face and neck to cover areas that stand out and catch more light (forehead, nose, cheekbones, chin, and ears) with a darker color such as loam or dark brown. Cover other areas, particularly recessed or shaded areas (around the eyes and under the chin), with lighter colors such as light green. Be sure to use an irregular pattern and do not use solid black, brown, or dark green as the only color. Face paint wears off over time, be disciplined and freshen up your camouflage. It is easy to let this slip as you sweat it off in the field. It is not enjoyable, but it is necessary to keep applying the camo paint as it wears off. Remember to keep your battle buddy up to speed in the field and always enforce camo discipline when you are a leader. Some will opt for face coverings as camouflage, these have their advantages however there are too many drawbacks for consistent use. Fogging of evepro as well as the fidget factor (constantly adjusting the face covering) can make these a non-starter. They are applicable if we must transition from the wilds to a more covert in plain sight environment during the same mission. Face coverings are the solution for this application as you will not want leftover signs of camo paint on your face or neck while blending in with the local street population.

It is a constant effort to keep face camo effective. There is nothing pleasant about re-applying camo paint, but we must have the discipline to keep it fresh.

Shine. As skin gets oily in the field, it becomes shiny. No matter your skin tone you must reduce shine by using camo paint (makeup) that we just discussed above. Equipment with worn off paint (and even some painted objects), if smooth, may still appear to shine. Glass objects such as mirrors, glasses, binoculars, and weapon mounted lights (WML) will shine. Cover these glass objects when not in use to avoid giving away your location. Cover shiny spots on equipment by painting, using lens covers or honeycomb, or wrapping with cloth or tape. Pay particular attention to covering boot eyelets, buckles on equipment, watches and GPS units, zippers, and any solid color object.

Shadow. When hiding or traveling, stay in the deepest part of the shadows. The outer edges of the shadows are lighter and the deeper parts are darker. If you are in an area where there is plenty of vegetation, keep as much vegetation as possible between you and a suspected enemy. Forcing an enemy to look through many layers of masking vegetation will fatigue his eyes quickly.

When traveling, especially in built-up areas at night, be aware of where you cast your shadow. It may extend out around the corner of a building and telegraph your position. If you are in dark shadow and there is a light source to one side, an enemy on the other side can see your silhouette against the light. Reading light under night vision is a critical skill, always use shadows and ambient lighting conditions to your advantage no matter if you are using NV or not. There is a tendency for newer NV users to move as if they can't be seen, this misperception of invisibility is a psychological bugaboo to guard against. Reading light and shadow under NV must be learned and practiced during training.

Scent. The longer an individual is away from civilization and modern plumbing the more sensitive they will be to human scent. A freshly showered person with clean clothes is easily detected in the woods, we must always camouflage the typical civilized scent associated with humans. Start by washing yourself with unscented soap and your clothes with a UV brightener free deer hunting specific detergent (or without using detergent at all). This washing method removes soap and body odors. Do not use tobacco products (best to break the habit now, even smokeless can be a detriment to a Scout). Weapons lubricants that have strong odor are also a risk, we all know how strong some brands of CLP smell. Pay attention to smells associated with humans such as fire, cigarettes, gasoline, oil, soap, and food (back to the SLLS practice). Depending on wind speed and direction such smells can alert you to human presence long before you can see or hear them. Note the wind's direction and, when possible, approach from the downwind side when nearing humans or an objective. This may be unpopular, but you may decide to not allow flameless ration heaters on a recon patrol during warmer months. The smell from these is unmistakable. During temperate months you should just resign yourself to eating unheated / body heated rations in the field when enemy contact is even remotely possible.

During freezing cold months, it will be unavoidable to heat rations and water, but caution is always in order. Don't directly heat or cook rations, the scent of the chow heating up and cooking will carry farther than just heating water and adding it to a freeze dried meal or putting an MRE pouch in hot water.

Flameless Ration Heaters (FRHs) can be a morale booster for chow in the field but they come with SLLS risks to the patrol. While they take very little water to activate an FRH is still consuming that precious resource as well.

Scout Gear and Equipment

This section highlights some of the equipment that is carried by Citizen Scouts, however this is not a comprehensive list. These items are not necessarily "special equipment" but they do warrant some additional discussion about the employment, setup, modification, or selection of a particular item and the associated capability for you as a Scout. Some items in this section are highlighted because of their utility for us as a Scout, items that are not necessarily special or "high speed" but have made life in the field much easier for us over the years.

The Scout Carbine. Our approach must always be one that is requirements driven and built in the context of the missions we anticipate. The GPR (General Purpose Rifle) and Recce Rifle terms have been a go-to in the community for a while now. These center on building a "one rifle" solution for the minuteman or Professional Citizen. The specific terms themselves are not the important piece; the critical part is using a requirements-based approach to build yourself something that works for most of your anticipated mission set. We will discuss this in specific titles and designations for long guns because that is the space the community is familiar with - we have become accustomed to hearing and building to "recce rifle" or "GPR" ideas so we will stick with that type of language to discuss some of the solutions. Don't get wrapped up in assigning a category or building a long gun to someone else's definition of success, the Scout Carbine concept in this section is just another option for you to consider. But at the end of the day, *always do what works for you.*

Some of the recce rifle builds we have seen in the community are truly outstanding. However, some have morphed into a gun optimized for roaming the wastelands while taking 800 meter keyhole shots at masked raiders. Some of these very capable guns are tipping the scale at 11 lbs plus...*unloaded.* Some recce rifle builds in the are so over-optimized or so over-generalized for unrealistic mission sets they cannot even meet the basic requirements we are discussing in this reference.

There are endless options the Scout can use to build a weapon system, many of which we covered in CM-1. No matter what you assess your use case /mission set to be, your long gun should be set up for general use. However, we must guard against it becoming *so* generalized that it actually becomes specialized. This is another one of those tactical paradoxes.

The Scout Carbine is akin to the CCW you currently carry. It will be carried a lot and shot a little. But as a Scout when you need it, you are **really** going to need it.

The Scout's mission requirements can drive the components and setup if you choose to optimize your long gun for a recon and security mission set. That being said, **we never build niche or one-off boutique guns for defensive use; *it must still serve you well across your entire mission set.*** We will not always have the luxury to make weapon choices as missions change. If you assess the bulk of your mission set to be along the lines of security, recon, and property patrols then a version of the Scout Carbine described in this section may be appropriate for you. But it must still be capable of conducting limited raids or ambushes and CQB tasks (which the proposed Scout Carbine setup described below can do). Keep this in mind as you consider this approach. Lightweight and capable, the Scout Carbine incorporates the CCW tenet of being a gun that is carried a lot and shot a little. But when you need it, you *really need it...* so it must be fully capable.

The Scout Carbine

Shooting is not the Scout's priority...until it is.

- ➤ Sub 7 lbs unloaded
- ➤ 13.7 to 16 inch 1:7 barrel
- ➤ RDS or HWS (passive NV capability)
- ➤ Two point adjustable sling
- ➤ Ability to attach a light (white or white/IR combo)

The same basics from the CM-1 weapons chapter apply; always start with a high-quality carbine. Paint it. Add a good two-point adjustable sling. Have a light (or the ability to quickly mount one). Mount an optic capable of being used with passive night vision. Train with it often and maintain it like a professional. If you deem you need an LPVO then by all means use an LPVO - just be aware of the weight penalty. If you need an IR laser - then add a laser. Just be aware of the weight penalty and probability of detection when using an active IR illuminator or laser. Suppressors can have a role in the Scout world, the use of these can confuse a threat as to the direction and distance of a shot and can make communication during an engagement a bit easier. Sometimes the weight, additional cleaning requirements, and length tradeoffs are worth adding a suppressor to a mission loadout - sometimes they are not. The choice is yours, just know what you are doing and why you are doing it. The Scout Carbine just happens to be "A" way that has worked for us very well.

You do you. If you think you need an LPVO, suppressor, or a bipod on your scout carbine then add them. Balance the tradeoffs and make it a deliberate decision – then go out and train with it.

Binoculars. Glass is a requirement for any reconnaissance mission. The eyeball only gets us so far. Having a magnified observation tool (binos, monocular, spotting scope, thermals) in a scout team is a requirement. Notice we didn't roll in a magnified rifle optic/LPVO in that list. Magnified weapon optics can definitely assist, but we need a dedicated off-weapon magnified piece of glass for observation. Rifle glass is great for target ID and

Magnified glass is a requirement for any reconnaissance mission. Ensure you have a magnified observation tool (binos, monocular, spotting scope) in your scout team loadouts.
photo courtesy of IG @RhodeIslandAboriginal

engagements, but they are not optimal for long term scanning and observation. A fixed power 8x or 10x waterproof binocular is optimal for magnified scanning and observation. This is sacrilege for glass snobs, but you don't need an overly expensive unit to meet this requirement. They just need to be durable, waterproof, and have good enough glass to get the job done.

Porro vs Roof Prism. We are not extreme bino experts, but we do know what features we need as a Scout and what works. We opt for roof prism models because they are typically more durable, lighter weight, and have better waterproof characteristics than porro prism models. By going with roof prism you will trade off field of view (comparing same specs between the two types) and cost as the roof prism models are usually more expensive for similar quality.

Power, Objective Lenses, FOV, and Exit Pupil. Many of the models you will consider will be between a magnification of 8 or 10. We recommend staying in the 7-10 range for magnification and getting a unit that is a fixed power.

Vortex 8x42 Roof Prism math shows an exit pupil diameter of 5.25mm (42 divided by 8 = 5.25mm). It indicates the size of the shaft of light that reaches your eyes, anything over 5mm is desired for lower light conditions. (Vortex catalog photo)

The higher the power the narrower the FOV (field of view is the width of the image you can see at 1,000 yards). The size of the objective lenses (the second number in model names) is a large determiner of how much light your binos can gather. Binoculars with larger objective lenses capture more light (when comparing similar spec units), providing you with a brighter image and more detail of the recon objective. Exit pupil size indicates the size of the shaft of light that reaches your eyes. A higher number indicates better viewing in low-light situations and is calculated by dividing the diameter of the objective lens by the magnification. For low-light situations, an exit pupil of 5mm or more is optimal, during limited visibility especially during BMNT and EENT having a high exit pupil number can make viewing easier.

No matter the FOV an 8x25, 8x40 and 8x42 pair of binoculars all provide the same magnification, the object will appear 8 times closer than it would to your naked eye.

Modifications. We recommend managing the signature of binos the same as you do for your long gun. Binos (or any optics) are tools you will use in relative proximity to the threat for extended duration. Glint from the objective lens, shine from an unpainted housing, or metal on metal of a bino frame hitting a carbine receiver are all risks for the Scout. Use the camouflage principles and the reverse SLLS assessment to modify your optics. Honeycomb objective covers or even 100mph tape with viewing slits over the objective lenses also works well to kill the glint. Painting the housing or attaching light scrim or burlap will cut the shine and out of place color of many handheld optics. Choosing rubberized models or using waterproof adhesive to attach burlap or cloth can help mitigate any metal-on-metal contact noise. These modifications must be done sparingly and not interfere with the function or maintenance of the optic, ensure you can access the glass for cleaning and maintenance and focus controls remain free.

Improve your equipment to make it work for you. Highly modified pair of 8x42 waterproof binos. Nothing rattles, nothing shines.

Monoculars are sub optimal for extended Scout use, the advantages of being light and small shrink in importance as they suffer from the same long duration use and field of view (FOV) challenges as the rifle optic. However, having a high quality 8 or 10x monocular for quick use can be an asset, as with all things mission will dictate what you add or subtract from your kit.

If you choose to have a monocular it should be supplementary, they should not be the only optic for the Scout.

Radio. A Scout must have the means to communicate; the only reason you are taking the risk of being out is to gather and pass along information. FM comms will most likely be high risk during a large-scale scenario due to direction finding and intercept capabilities of even a slightly sophisticated threat. The selection is less about which radio to buy and train on but more about choosing when and where to push to talk. Yes, we must choose hardware carefully, many of the cheaper radios are not going to hold up to the rigors of scouting. But that is a onetime decision, after selecting a radio that is waterproof (water resistant at a minimum) and meets the frequency and use requirements the challenge is all knowledge based.

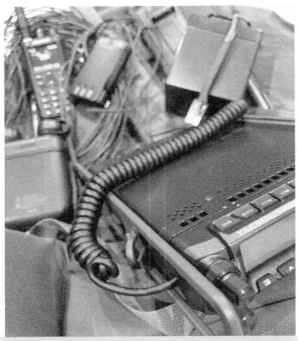

Radio systems for the Scout must be robust and power efficient. HF systems may be part of your plan as well. No matter what system, be judicious with transmissions due to the threat of direction finding and intercept of the actual message.

After understanding the threat and vulnerabilities Scout teams must select and employ the systems to send reports. These may include the handheld (HT) systems that all of us own, more robust HTs that might have encryption capability, or HF systems capable of reaching command posts out of UHF/VHF range. Scouts are unique in they must be comms experts, even more so than a "standard" fire team member. Selection and employment of specific antennas, terrain masking, and leveraging atmospheric conditions to enhance or conceal transmissions are all skills the Scout needs. This is always more than a hardware discussion, we cannot simply "buy the capability" for the communications component. Our comms requirements are well beyond blister pack FRS radios. There is a ton of comms and hardware information available (some good, some bad...and a *lot* of gatekeeping). Always use caution when sifting through it and apply your critical thinking skills to what folks are saying.

Power management will always be a challenge for the Scout operating away from the grid. Recharging in the field during a mission via solar is not a great option for our requirements. In our experience light and compact systems take far too long to charge devices and good systems are too bulky to carry along with all of our other gear. We have found it more efficient to carry battery packs or just a spare set of batteries vs going solar. Understanding, tracking, and managing power consumption individually (and in your team) will ensure you have enough power in reserve when you need it.

Navigation Tools. Every Scout must have a high-quality set of navigation tools with redundant options. Do not cut corners when selecting your nav equipment. Weatherproof, durable, and proven are the watchwords for these items.

Compass. The standard for a Scout's primary compass should be a US military lensatic compass. Note I did not say "military style" compass, this instrument is critical and must be a proven one. Current NSN (National Stock

Number, this means the military has approved it for purchase) lensatic compasses are the recommended choice for your primary. Tritium or phosphorescent is your choice, each has its advantages. A backup compass can be either another lensatic or a smaller, lighter baseplate compass. Having a small and light baseplate stashed in a shoulder or cargo pocket is a smart move. The caution here is never select an off-brand baseplate compass to save a couple of bucks. Silva, Suunto, and Brunton are all trusted brands. Within these you will find different models that may or may not work for you. Get some experience in the field with your choice and it will become evident if you like a particular model. Some baseplates, even the well-built ones, may not have phosphorescent markings. We recommend choosing a model that has them so it can be used at night.

A small watchband or wrist compass can be a contingency item, but these should not be second in line in case your lensatic clocks out on you. The PACE (Primary, Alternate, Contingency, Emergency) system applies to navigation tools as well.

A backup compass is a must, the baseplate is a good option for your alternate. Choose a reputable manufacturer and pick a model that has phosphorescent markings for night use.

Chest Rigs and Load Bearing Equipment (LBE).
The Scout can be served well by either (depending on preference and mission). Mission, duration, the type of terrain, personal preference, vehicle use, and weather will all influence this choice. The loadout discussion from earlier will drive your decision of how you choose to carry your gear and ammo, but the Scout will have to apply some additional thought to the positives and negatives of the different options for their role in a recon mission. Choosing one may drive you to add other components (assault packs) to carry the needed equipment. NV devices and shelter may easily ride in an LBE or a Smersh, but with the limited real estate on a typical chest rig you will have to find other means to carry them such as a Camelbak™ or a small assault pack you can IMT with. Temps and weather will drive the requirement as well, even in warmer daytime temps a stationary night can turn from uncomfortable to deadly without proper protection from the elements.

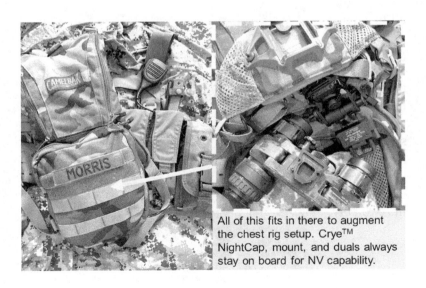

All of this fits in there to augment the chest rig setup. Crye™ NightCap, mount, and duals always stay on board for NV capability.

The LBE is *still* the optimal choice for longer range and duration dismounted recon work. This may be an unpopular position for some people, but for our mission set as a dismounted irregular force with limited resupply the LBE (or similar type setups) is the optimal choice. This is not to say that another solution won't work for you, but for the missions in this manual and the anticipated sustainment challenges the LBE setup will work best. Chest rigs, plate carriers, vest systems all have their place, especially for shorter duration missions such as property patrols. But the load carriage real estate runs out much faster on those and can leave sustainment and shelter requirements unmet. Everything from modern belt kits to old school ALICE LBE can be used, or a mix of old and new. Even with the surplus kit going up in price ALICE still costs a fraction of some of the modern takes on the same concept. Is it old? You bet it is. With modifications and some updates we think it is worth considering if you don't

want to go all in on a new production model. The takeaway is new or old the belt and suspender load bearing system is here to stay.

For dismounted recon missions some form of a Load Bearing system is best. New or old doesn't matter, use what works for you that will carry enough sustainment and shelter to get you through.

Field Jacket Liner. The M65 field jacket liner is a hidden gem that we have used as a layering system for decades. The field jacket is not worthy of field use, but the liner sure is. A light base layer of merino or polypro (even just a performance T shirt) with the field jacket liner over it and the BDU/utility top over the liner is outstanding down into the high 40s (other factors notwithstanding). Not too bulky, comfortable to wear, still retains *some* warmth if it does happen to get wet and is inexpensive. Layering the field jacket liner under gore tex jackets is also good to go. A bit too warm to use during a movement, but once you stop they are outstanding to retain some heat. Fortunately, there is an abundance of US mil spec ones available, the relatively newer models even have built in buttons for closure. We have plenty of new fabric technology options we use as well, but for the price this may be a great option for you as part of your system. Jay talks more about layering in the CM-9, whatever you choose just have options you can add or subtract to regulate temp and prevent cold weather sweating.

The old school M-65 Field Jacket Liner is an inexpensive layer option that can serve you well for years to come. Layer this under your outer blouse/shirt when stationary in the cooler temps.

Crevat. These are one of the best daytime headgear options for a Scout when conducting dismounted, stealthy reconnaissance in eastern woodlands, jungle, and temperate forests. Boonie hats (or any hat with a brim) will create reflection and some refraction resulting in minor echo or distortion as sounds come into the ear. While not incredibly significant this slight change in sound delivery can influence which direction a distant or low sound seems to come from. Don't get me wrong, boonies are still a great option especially for sun protection, but don't dismiss cravat use as an option for times when NV mounting solutions or ballistic helmets are not required to be worn. And of course there is zero ballistic protection, so smart METT-TC tradeoffs apply as always.

The cravat is a great item for a Scout to have. Use as a head wrap / drive on rag to keep the echoes down. Comfortable to wear in high heat and humidity, but no ballistic protection so use accordingly.

Bivy cover. This one should be mandatory for your team's packing list, it can save your life. Relatively light and packs down to a tolerable size the bivy will protect you from rain and snow. Sometimes you can get away with no shelter construction if you have a bivy, it isn't hotel room comfy or warm, but it will keep you as dry as possible in a field environment.

The outer Gore Tex bivy of the Military Sleep System (MSS) is light and can be packed easily. Just having the bivy (the camouflaged cover in the photo) can be a lifesaver.

It is the outer layer to build on (in) for sleep systems and should be a priority purchase and priority to carry. Surplus in new old stock condition used to be inexpensive, they have shot up in price a good bit but don't let that delay you getting one. Be very picky about condition, a leaky bivy defeats the purpose. The internet surplus store "in fair condition" ACU pattern bivy for 60 bucks will be a leaky nightmare in the cold rain. There are some great commercial versions as well, do your research to be sure they are good to go for quality and your requirements. Outdoor Research and MSR each have great options, just know that you are going to be in the $200 range for commercial versions and for very good or new condition military surplus you will still pay around $150-$200 (as of publication date).

Camouflage Material

Pieces of camo netting stashed in a ruck, a small roll of netting, or "sniper veils" are examples of camo material you may take on a mission. Use these items to assist in camouflaging static positions or OPs, it will save you time and will offset the requirement to move vegetation around to camo your hide site or OP. Exercise caution when using these, the netting especially. Movement can be exaggerated and transferred to a larger surface area if these coverings are employed improperly. Using big chunks of netting as scrim while on patrol is also ill-advised due to the movement and issues. Remember that we can get away with a few more camouflage indicator sins if we keep our movement and noise minimized. *Wrapping your carbine with netting or material is not advised*, as we discussed earlier just paint it and drive on. Tarps, space blankets, and ponchos can afford

Small sections of camo net or mesh sniper veils are useful to cover gear and help camouflage positions. Be judicious in their use, we recommend using only when stationary.

some overhead concealment and weather protection, but they can look out of place if done improperly. Thermal camouflage is also a consideration, but that is a whole other challenge for us that we will address in later manuals.

Deliberate Observation

Scouts go out with a well-defined purpose that supports either your self-directed mission or the unit's mission. There are several doctrinal terms that help frame what we look for on the battlefield and more importantly *why*. Some of the common terms in the reconnaissance and intelligence communities are below. These may seem very foreign, or you may think these terms don't really apply to you doing a one-man property patrol. If you are familiar with the doctrine, you understand that many of these apply only to larger units with commanders and staff. These are terms and concepts that are developed and pushed down from command level organizations; however, you need to be familiar with them because you will 1. hear the terms during training and operations and 2. you should understand them and be able to adapt them for your use. Even if they don't pass the uptight doctrine weenie test for use at your level, we must adapt them to the conditions we will face. I would encourage you to dig into these a bit. The terms can seem irrelevant, but when you unpack the concepts you will find they still be applicable as a homeowner just looking to secure their corner of the neighborhood. These terms and concepts start to build complexity, but as a Scout you must always associate these with the "why" you are out doing what you are doing - so we will discuss a few of them here in the foundational Scout chapter.

PIR (Priority Intelligence Requirement) is an intelligence requirement about the enemy (a piece of specific information) that the leader must have to understand the threat and other aspects of the operational environment. PIR focuses us to answer questions about the enemy to confirm actions. PIR becomes the central focus for scouts conducting reconnaissance and security. There are other relationships of elements that become a swirling mass of acronyms (PIR are part of CCIR, there is EEFI and FFIR, SIR etc etc etc). It can get complicated to say the least, so for us we will leave the discussion at PIR for now. What I want you to take away from this is you are out scouting and looking for a reason, observing with a purpose. If you are executing a self-directed mission make sure you have done your homework and be self-aware of the specific "why" your unit is going out.

There is no standard for PIRs, but good ones ask only one question and focus on a specific fact, event, or activity. They ask a question in a manner that when answered, will provide a piece of information required to support a single decision. As a simple example *"Will the enemy conduct ground resupply of fuel along Avenue of Approach 2 (COPPERHEAD ROAD)?"* Good PIR are "yes" or "no" questions, simplifying the information requirement to confirm or deny the presence of a variable.

NAI (Named Area of Interest). An NAI is an area where information that will answer a PIR can be collected. This is a place where the presence or absence of something will confirm or deny an enemy course of action. When we say "deny" in this case it does not indicate we will prevent something, it just means what we observe will either prove (confirm) what we thought the enemy was going to do or it would deny (disprove) our assessment of their actions. From our earlier fuel truck PIR example, we would know that the best place to look for indicators that will answer the PIR (fuel tanker route selection) is the intersection of RTE 460 and COPPERHEAD ROAD. *Everything a Scout does is to support decision making*, an NAI is a specific "go look here for this thing to confirm or deny what we think the enemy will do" to put it in extremely simple terms.

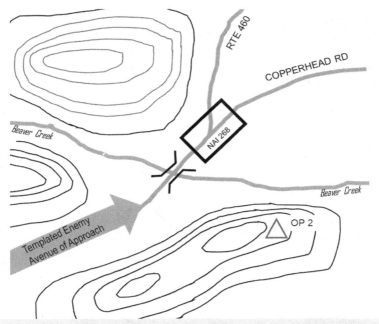

Scouts at OP2 observing NAI 268 would report if the enemy sends fuel trucks north on RTE 460 or East on Copperhead Rd (or both). This can confirm or deny an enemy action from our prior mission planning and will cause the leader (potentially you) to make a decision with your forces.

DP (Decision Point) is a point in space and time when you or your leader anticipates making a key decision concerning a friendly (your) course of action. A decision point is associated with actions by the enemy, the friendly force, or the population, and it is tied to a specific commander's critical information requirement (CCIR). A Decision Point is the military equivalent of the "if/then" statement; if or when this happens, I will do this. The graduate level work is figuring out the details for these DPs so you can stay ahead of the threat. We refer to this as getting inside the enemy's decision cycle - we are anticipating and making decisions and executing faster than him. The art and science behind this process is extensive, just understand that everything we are driving toward in this manual is to support a leader to be able to make sound, timely decisions.

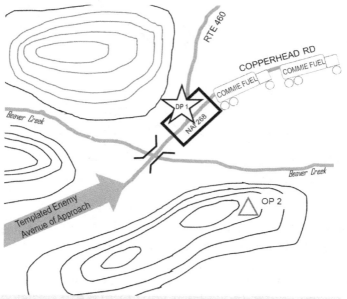

Fuel trucks take the right fork down COPPERHEAD ROAD, so actions in NAI 268 indicate fuel resupply is headed East and have answered the PIR. Criteria for DP1 (Decision Point 1) has also been met for the leader to make the execution decision (predetermined in the plan, perhaps it is to have his forces execute a preplanned ambush along the route).

So now we have some understanding of the big picture and why we go out to recon, we will discuss the mechanics and details of how we go about it. A Scout observes the environment to establish a baseline and identify anomalies or indicators. There are three requirements for this observation process to work: light, motion, and edges. Your eye must receive light (either natural or amplified) to form an image, motion to prevent the stimulus from fading away, and edges to preclude vision fade and disorientation. These components are mildly interesting when listed like this, but they give you some basic elements that will assist with learning the specifics of how and what to look for when conducting recon and surveillance.

Look with a purpose. You are there to gather facts and provide information that will either confirm or deny a specific enemy action. Information gathered by the individual is reported, analyzed, and processed into intelligence for use by the group intel cell. You may just be gathering info for your family, the squad or patrol leader if the squad is operating independently, but the principles and methodology is the same.

When observing an area, Scouts will establish a *baseline* from an initial look or assessment of the subject you are looking at. It is a mindful, intentional first look you will use to establish what is normal state. You will then use it for comparison at a later time. We do this in everyday life, but it is done mostly on an unconscious level. The "well, that ain't right" moment when you see a puddle of coolant under your truck is a good example. The difference is most times we aren't intentionally checking for the coolant leak each time we approach our personal vehicle. We just happen to notice the leak because it is an anomaly (out of the norm) for us, it is a change from our baseline.

For the Scout this baseline process is intentional; you are mentally "locking in" and taking notes on normal (current state) of the observed area in detail. An initial set of critical observations or data that is used to establish what is normal for comparison at another time, a baseline is dynamic that will continually evolve. Everything has a baseline, especially the human environment. Scouts establish a baseline by looking at the current situation, context, and relevance of their observations. Ok this sounds silly, but do you remember as a kid doing those "spot the difference" picture games? There would be one drawing on the left that depicted a scene (the baseline) and then one on the right that had 10 differences. Those differences are only relevant because you had the original baseline to compare it to. Same concept, just higher stakes and you weren't calling in a SPOTREP to your kindergarten teacher.

After recording (notes and sketch) and reporting your initial observations, changes from this baseline are what you are looking for. How many windows are open this morning on the building? Are there four or five antennas on the roof today? Did the generator get refilled two or three times before 1900 today? Did they fill it with yellow jerry cans or pump from a 5,000-gallon white fuel truck this time? It is the presence, absence, or change of something that creates a deviation from the baseline. We need to reiterate that scouts must not over-interpret what they see and report their conclusions, they report facts. Scout experience will guide which seemingly mundane facts are reported (unless they are part of the PIR for that particular objective). Experience and leader guidance will determine what is worthy of recording. Some changes are irrelevant, some observed changes from the baseline can decide significant changes in a friendly COA. This is the art and science of being a Scout.

Scouts will most definitely provide assessments of the situation to their leadership, but these assessments must be identified clearly as such and be separated from the facts. The leadership or intelligence cells will process the raw information to paint the full picture. Remember if you are operating independently – the person doing all this assessment is you or your SL.

Scouts must be able to *recall* the most important details that are required for identification or assessment. Training scouts using the Keep In Memory (KIM) game is an effective training technique. In broad terms a KIM game consists of several (10 is a good baseline) items on a table, covered with a blanket or poncho. Scouts observe the objects when uncovered but cannot touch an item, take notes, or talk during the exercise. After a prescribed time, the items are covered, and the team members write their observations on a score sheet. They write the details that accurately describe the object, omitting unnecessary words. There are variations that can be incorporated into a KIM game, such as an extended amount of time between observing and recording what was seen, induce distractions while observing and recording, or the use of different methods to display items.

So how do we observe an area as a Scout to make sure we see everything?

The Observation Process. Observation begins with the gathering and processing of information obtained through the senses. Scouts must train their five senses for the task and environment, it is almost re-learn as you focus the senses for your role as a Scout.

Observation Techniques. Observation techniques include the *Hasty Search, the Detailed Search, and Maintaining Observation.*

Example of a Hasty Search
(upon occupying or stopping at a position)

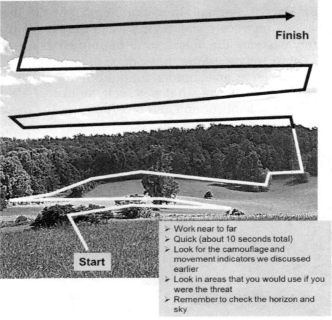

Finish

Start

> Work near to far
> Quick (about 10 seconds total)
> Look for the camouflage and movement indicators we discussed earlier
> Look in areas that you would use if you were the threat
> Remember to check the horizon and sky

Hasty Search. The hasty search is the first phase of observing a target area. Upon occupying your concealed position conduct a hasty search for any threat activity (or any activity at all). This should only take a few seconds. The hasty search is carried out by making quick glances at specific points, terrain features, or other areas that may conceal a threat. Do not sweep your eyes across the terrain in one continuous movement, this will prevent you from detecting motion. View the area closest to your position first and work near to far (the sky is scanned from the horizon back to the observer as you continue the scan). We do this as a best practice since relative ground threat distance from near to far *usually* presents the most immediate threat. Continue the visual search further out until the entire target area is scanned.

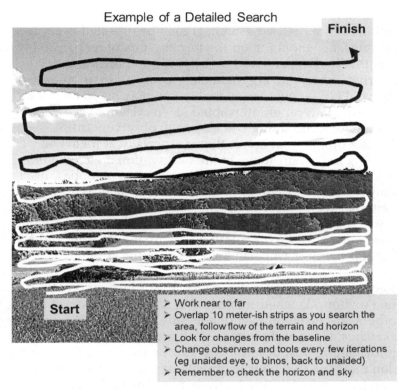

Example of a Detailed Search

Finish

Start

➤ Work near to far
➤ Overlap 10 meter-ish strips as you search the area, follow flow of the terrain and horizon
➤ Look for changes from the baseline
➤ Change observers and tools every few iterations (eg unaided eye, to binos, back to unaided)
➤ Remember to check the horizon and sky

Detailed Search. After the hasty search, you start a detailed search using the overlapping strip method. Again, since the area nearest the observer offers the greatest danger begin your detailed search there. Systematically search the terrain from your right (or left) flank in a 180-degree arc, 50 meters in depth. After reaching the opposite flank, the searches the next area nearest your OP or hide site. The search should be in overlapping strips of at least 10 meters to ensure total coverage of the area. The detailed search should cover as far out as you can see, with the aid of an optic device, always including areas of interest that attracted the observer during the hasty search.

Maintaining Observation. The observer must memorize as much of the area as possible. A cycle of a hasty search, followed by a detailed search, should be repeated every few minutes, depending upon the terrain, area of responsibility and the level of perceived activity. A best practice is to alternate observers approximately every 20 to 30 minutes to avoid eye fatigue, but in reality you may be on for a few hours to allow an uninterrupted sleep cycle for your Scout teammate(s). Rotating will also keep observers from "seeing things" that aren't there (especially at night) or missing important items in the observation area. Scouts will burn out quickly if they keep their eyes on optics, not only should we rotate between observers we also want to swap between tools (binos, thermals, naked eye). At night it will require close management to stay alert and maintain observation. Observer rotation and mixing thermal and NV (as appropriate) will also help alleviate the strain.

Record and Report Observations. Record what you observe in a written/sketched manner that can be understood by others and fused into actionable intelligence. Using notes, sketches, video and photos are all means to capture the information. Just because you know a piece of information don't assume that your teammate or your leadership knows that same info. Writing instruments, Rite in the Rain notebooks, sketch kits, thermal devices with on board recording, and cameras to support the recording. If time allows, develop a terrain sketch as a reference or to pass on to your higher HQ or to the next scout team that may relieve you and occupy the OP. Observation reporting is conducted in the SALUTE or SALT format, so this is a familiar task for you. There is nothing special about the format a scout uses, they are just very precise and proficient at using them. Having a way to record what you observe seems obvious, but you would be surprised how many inexperienced observers will not have the most basic of tools (a waterproof notebook and a pencil or pen).

Observation Posts (OP)

What is an OP? An observation post (OP) is a static, concealed position that either provides early warning for a defensive position/fixed site/neighborhood or it gathers information while observing a recon objective. A recon or security mission may require the team to occupy a position to observe an area or a threat. OPs provide early warning of impending enemy contact by reporting direction, distance, and size (Contact reports followed by SPOTREPs). Scouts running OPs detect the enemy early and send accurate reports to their leaders or higher unit to gain time for those leaders to make tactical decisions. These positions can range from a hasty position, which a team may use for a few hours, to a more permanent position, which the team could occupy for a few days. One quick note, an OP can be manned by anyone, not just a scout. We are focusing on Scouts in this section, but I don't want to cause confusion or indicate that an OP is a scout specific "thing". Scouts man OPs with a minimum of two and will occupy an OP for a few minutes up to three days or so. Sometimes you will hear the term "LP/OP" which means Listening Post / Observation Post. Units over the years have taken liberty with the definitions and how they are employed, so you may be familiar with discussions about LPs being split out and doing different tasks in relation to OPs or other variations that change roles based on lighting or weather conditions. For our purposes we will keep the concept simple and just refer to them as OP.

Offensive (Reconnaissance) vs Defensive (Security) OPs. This differentiation is not Army/USMC doctrine by any means, so be warned this concept is specific to our Citizen / nonstandard way of looking at the problem set. An OP is an OP is an OP - however for our purposes it may make sense to distinguish these two general applications considering the resource challenges of our small units (both personnel and material). This difference can be one of hasty vs deliberate OPs, or surface vs subsurface but it makes more sense for us to mentally differentiate based on the purpose (recon vs security) they support.

Observation Posts supporting defensive or security missions of a stationary force are established along the most likely enemy avenues of approach (the routes they are most likely to take) into the defensive position or your area of operation. These will most likely be subsurface OPs. Consider your neighborhood, your homestead, apartment complex etc and imagine spots where you could observe an approaching threat. Always tie this in with the terrain analysis you learned from CM-1 (OAKOC) to figure out the best places to observe from.

Where would you place an OP to observe the high speed avenue of approach (the hardball road) coming into town? (everything East of Salt Creek is enemy controlled or unknown)

An observation post is a concealed "lookout post" that provides the primary early warning in the defense by reporting direction, distance, and size of any threat. While we never want to have a reactive mindset (vs a proactive one), the OP supporting the defense or a stationary activity is indeed a bit more reactive in nature. Detailed discussion of defensive operations is beyond the scope of this manual. Just know that there are different planning factors and requirements for static or defensive focused OP emplacement (these are not "guard posts" nor should they be treated as such). Providing early warning and information to a stationary friendly force or area is the purpose of these. For our requirements a series of pre-planned OPs makes sense for providing early warning to your sanctuary or neighborhood. The layered defenses of family units and fixed site areas is an effective way to protect families, the group's safe shelter, and resources. Interior guards and checkpoints or Entry Control Points (ECPs) supported by an outer ring of defensive oriented OPs and security patrols, and finally active combat patrols to provide the outer layer. The static OPs in the middle layer can be pre-planned prior to X Hour based on METT-TC analysis and your IPB process and then adjusted as the situation changes. There is a disadvantage in that they will eventually be templated or discovered by a threat, however there are ways to protect the longevity of the system. While this is worth mentioning for context, the details are beyond our discussion in here.

OPs supporting offensive or recon missions / surveillance tasks are used to observe enemy or templated enemy positions that are defined as recon objectives or NAIs. These are typically surface, however they can be semi-subsurface as well depending on conditions and time. Scouts may occupy OPs during these missions to gather information about an enemy activity relative to the terrain. Remember occupying the OP is not the mission, what you are looking at and reporting back is the mission. You will have to adjust locations based on the changing situation, this is where the mission type orders apply. As you already know even the "lowest" level fighter will have to make adjustment decisions to support the purpose of the larger mission. The optimal OP number is 3 to 5, because it affords enough Scouts to have an R team (Recon) to recon/observe the NAI and an S team (Security) to provide security for the R team. Additionally, there are enough fighters to react to direct fire contact, ground evac wounded personnel while still being able to fight as a team, and carry all necessary equipment to observe, report, and a bit more combat power if engaged by a threat. Any higher than 5 in a single OP increases chance of compromise.

The urgency of sending reports back will be guided by the situation and leader's recon guidance. Again, this offense/defense role and purpose differentiation is a non-doctrinal categorization of OPs, but it may help you keep the associated requirements straight in your mind.

Early detection reduces the risk of the enemy overrunning an observation post of either category. OPs may be equipped with passive night vision, thermals, unmanned systems (drones and even ground systems), acoustic, or frequency detecting sensors to increase its ability to detect the enemy. You may have devices that provide warning such as electronic or tripwire systems. There is a tradeoff with using the loud 209 shotgun primer/.22 blank tripwire devices as they will not only alert you, but they can also indicate our presence to the threat. They can be triggered by larger game animals which brings its own set of challenges for the scout teams so employ these after determining the risk.

The patrol leader will weigh the advantages and disadvantages of using infrared illumination. It is a safe assumption that any threat will have some form of light amplifying NV. Reports from the southern US border as of publication date indicate that cartels are well equipped and are infiltrating with high power IR laser/illuminators and current generation passive night vision systems.

To further reduce the risk of fratricide, observation posts must accurately navigate to the exit and entry point in the higher unit's position. The leader ensures he submits an observation post location to the command post/ friendly units in the area to ensure a No Fire Area (NFA) is established around each observation post position.

Some characteristics of a good Observation Post

Covered and concealed ingress and egress routes. Scouts must be able to enter and leave the OP without being seen by the enemy.

Unobstructed observation of the assigned area or sector. Ideally, the fields of observation of adjacent OPs (if present) overlap to ensure full coverage of the sector.

Cover and concealment. OP positions have cover and concealment to reduce their vulnerability. You may need to pass up a position with favorable observation of the objective that has no cover and concealment and select a new position affording better survivability.

Defensive OPs must still be concealed and low profile even though they will have enhanced survivability. Exposed OPs like this one along the Korean DMZ will become bullet (or worse) magnets when there is an attack.

In a concealed location that does not attract attention. OPs should not be sited in locations with distinguishable features such as a radio tower, an isolated grove of trees, or a lone building. These positions might draw enemy attention and will most likely be used as enemy artillery Targets or an enemy direct fire TRP (Target Reference Point). Scouts may need to pass up a position with favorable observation attributes but has little cover and concealment.

Positioned so that will not skyline the observers. Avoid hilltops and position OPs further down the slope of the hill or on the side, provided there are covered and concealed routes into and out of the position. METT-TC applies as always, think through the entirety of the problem set as you down-select where you will observe from. To preserve security an OP should be located no closer than 300 meters from the objective area. 300 meters it sounds like a long way, but that is close for an OP. Your guys occupying one that close will have a hard time staying undetected for more than a few hours.

Don't get trapped. I can't over emphasize this one. You must leave yourself a way out by selecting terrain that supports your self-extraction if you are compromised. Choosing terrain that prevents you and your team from slipping away during enemy contact is not what we want. We do not have the means to fight a protracted engagement if we are compromised. Unless friendly US forces can cut some support assets to you the AH-64s aren't coming to save the day. Choosing a location that will allow you to quickly put a major terrain feature between you and an enemy without getting boxed in is tactically sound. A Scout's nightmare is getting cut off from his squad or platoon while being pursued by a determined threat. Balancing this risk and the mission requirements always demands graduate level planning. Don't misinterpret this point, we can't be risk averse or paralyzed by over analysis of this - sometimes you just get stuck with a piece of bad ground. Preserving the quick and agile guerilla force attributes discussed earlier in this manual must always be prioritized and supported in our planning. Do your best to avoid terrain that is a disadvantage if possible.

Stay in range of supporting direct fire. Standard practice for a conventional unit is OPs should be placed no further than half maximum effective range of the friendly weapon system (of the next higher unit to the rear of the OP or OP line) such as an Entry Control Point (ECP).

If the line of sight is less than the maximum effective range, then it should be no further than half the distance of the farthest visible point. However, this will likely not apply to our units when we are out on missions, our dispersion will be greater and assets will be fewer than a conventional unit. We must operate with what we have, so adjust your plans to leverage the strengths of your units and minimize the weaknesses. In a static position / defensive optimized role the OP or series of OPs should follow this "half max effective range" guideline to allow support from the stationary force.

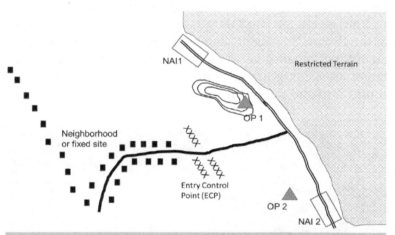

Rudimentary sketch of how defense oriented OPs are integrated and supported by the parent unit. OP 1 and 2 are located no more than half the effective direct fire weapons range (small arms) from the unit manning the checkpoint/ECP.

Planning an OP

Based on commander's recon guidance, directed OP locations, and mission analysis the patrol leader selects the *general* location for OPs via map recon. After analyzing METT-TC factors the patrol leader determines how many OPs must be established. The leader uses topo maps, aerial photos, visual recon before the mission, and information gained from prior missions or other units operating in the area. The patrol leader decides where the OPs must be generally positioned to allow long-range observation along the avenues of approach or NAIs assigned by his commander (or solely determined during mission analysis if your small unit is operating independently). The team leader on an OP will select the final position on the ground once they arrive on the site. Scout team leaders must understand the intent and have good terrain sense as they will be selecting a site that will be within observation range of the threat. The Scout team ensures the position provides an optimal balance between maximum observation of the target area, concealment from enemy observation, covered routes into and out of the position.

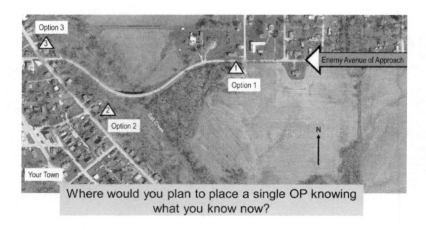

Where would you plan to place a single OP knowing what you know now?

There are many factors that we must leave out for brevity's sake and this is just a 2D flat satellite photo - but let's take a shot at the OP placement exercise from the figure on the previous page.

Option 1 (No Go) - Good line of sight down the hardball road, but the OP is exposed to the enemy and is potentially out of direct fire support range from the friendly positions (in town). Most importantly the Scouts in OP1 would have their backs to a river with only a single exposed crossing point to get back to friendlies. Hard pass for this Scout.

Option 2 (not great, not terrible) – Scouts can observe the bridge crossing along the avenue of approach. Very limited line of sight to the East, they can see the bridge but there is a missed opportunity to see the enemy earlier (eg farther East). Close enough for wire comms (field phone) or even hand / visual signals. Option 2 is OK, but there is another better option.

Option 3 (the Best Option) – Scouts have the same line of sight as option 1 but aren't trapped on the wrong side of the river. They can detect a threat long before they get to the bridge. OP3 has good escape routes back into the town without being exposed to the east, close enough use field phone/wire comms, great line of sight, and keeps an existing obstacle between them and the majority of the threat. Option 3 is the best option (this is a simplified discussion of course; far more factors will come into play for you on the ground when doing it for real).

Occupying the OP

During the mission planning phase, the Scout TL conducts a map recon and selects an objective rally point (ORP) short of the OP ("short" means it is on the friendly side, the

99

proposed OP site you are going to is between the ORP and the objective). From this ORP, the team recons the tentative position to determine the exact location of its final OP. The location of the ORP should provide cover and concealment from enemy fire and observation, be located as close to the selected area as possible and have good routes into and out. From the ORP, the team moves forward to a point that allows them to view the tentative OP. Depending on the mission, the situation, size of the team, and duration you may leave a security team in the ORP while the recon teams disperse to recon the objectives.

After you have located the templated OP do not take a direct route into it. Just like a patrol base, use a button hook or dog leg route to move to a position that allows viewing the OP to make sure it is clear of enemy. Scout(s) remain in this location to overwatch the Scout who recons the area to decide the final OP position. Once a suitable OP location has been set the covering team member(s) joins their fellow Scout at the position. This last process we just described is not over great distances, the overwatch is close by. He is most likely in pistol range...but the process is still a deliberate one. While conducting the recon or moving to the position the team moves slowly and intentionally. Use high or low crawl techniques and avoid unnecessary movement of trees, bushes, and grass. Conduct those micro SLLS halts we talked about before and be especially vigilant since you are approaching a position your team will occupy for a relatively extended time. Being this close to the final position the slower you move and the more careful you are, the better. Observe a section of your route before you move along it, avoid making any noise, and stay in the shadows. Be careful not to disturb or cut any vegetation unless absolutely necessary to gain observation of your assigned objective/NAI.

Using the cover of night to occupy the OP may be advantageous, but you may have to adjust the location after sunrise to account for issues you may not have seen at night. It is a balancing act, the advantages of one condition (cover of night) may become disadvantages later (daytime can reveal the position is not as concealed as you originally thought).

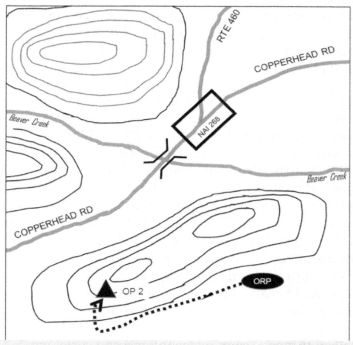

Never go directly to the OP; always consolidate at an ORP at a covered and concealed position on the friendly side of a terrain feature. Approach the OP by an indirect route to conduct the initial recon and final siting of the position.

When your Scout team arrives at the OP, you will conduct a hasty then detailed search of the target area just as we described earlier in this section. Ensure security first, last, and always; the team is especially vulnerable when it moves into a new area for the first time.

Manning and OP Activities

A minimum of two scouts man each OP (4-5 is may be better, but it depends on the situation). They must be equipped to observe, report, protect themselves, and call for assistance from their parent unit. One scout observes the area while the other provides local security, records information, and sends reports to the section/squad leader or platoon leader. The two scouts should switch jobs every 20 to 30 minutes because the observer's effectiveness decreases quickly after that time. Sleep plans, water resupply, battery management are all things that must be carefully planned. There will be no opportunity for the team to "take a break", once they occupy the OP, they remain there until displacement criteria is met (enemy actions, trigger points, timelines per the OPORD etc). Being on a 72 hour OP can be abject misery at times, even with the manpower to rotate tasks (try to limit recon mission OP occupation to under 24 hours to prevent compromise). Leaders must plan accordingly as two-man OP effectiveness degrades quickly and should be limited to just a few hours. Weather and hours of darkness can also negatively affect the efficiency and longevity of the team. A third or fourth Scout will allow that timeline to stretch to 24 hours and beyond, but only if you have the right team members with proper training and discipline.

We talked through scanning techniques and switching observers and devices, but we need to highlight some aspects of the human element. The adrenaline dump of being in relatively close contact with a threat in a hopefully one-sided hide and seek can quickly fade into complacency. This level of complacency can grow as we get cold, tired, and hungry. Scout leaders must be aware of their team's mental state and level of fatigue, any slip up could result in a compromise.

Staring at a human. Some of you may have heard this before, this phenomenon is not urban legend and is well known inside the reconnaissance community. Do not stare directly at another human being when you are observing. That freaky sixth-sense thing? Yes, it really is a thing. Odds are if you stare directly at another human for any amount of time, even through optics, they will get the sense that someone is watching them. Best practice is always moving your gaze off or around a bit even at distance. No need to go crazy with it, just be aware that this phenomenon is an absolute unscientific truth.

When rotating observation duties, special equipment should remain in place, and the optics are handed from one member to the other. Scout data books, observation logs, range cards, and the radio should be placed where both members have easy access to them to minimize movement in the OP. All latrine calls should be done during darkness, if possible. A cat hole should be dug to conceal any traces of latrine calls and preserve field hygiene.

The team starts priorities of work and improves the position or starts construction of the OP if required (more on this in a bit). The Scouts organize their equipment so that it is easily accessible without making noise (as a quick aside the consequence of using hook and loop closures will become apparent as you try to silently remove necessary items for use). Establish a system of observing, eating, resting, and latrine calls to rotate in fresh sets of eyes for the duration. The comms plan (using the PACE methodology) is put in place to include antenna emplacement in the comms location (do not transmit FM from the OP site due to the risk of direction finding). Depending on the situation and your team size / SOP you may establish a hide site to the rear of the OP to allow

Scouts to rotate off the OP. This site is not a everybody go chill out zone. Security, priorities of work, light, noise and litter discipline must be to standard, but a hide site can give a bit of relief out of line of sight from the objective.

As we shift into night hours our passive NV and thermal systems become a requirement (quick reminder that thermals are not for night only, they are a 24 hour tool depending on conditions). Light amplification devices (NV) allow the scout to detect threats at reasonable distances under the right conditions, but they have range challenges. Having a thermal capability on a team to supplement is creeping into the mandatory requirement territory for the Citizen organization. Having a thermal sight or thermal monocular on a team will significantly enhance a scout's capability, especially when occupying an OP.

No matter what tools you have the frequent rotation of observers and cycling of methods (switching from naked eye to binos or thermals and back again) is important to prevent observer burnout. We can't keep our eyeballs buried in glass for extended periods of time.

Take every opportunity to rest, but do not sacrifice security. Rotate security so that all members of your team can rest. Security trumps comfort every time, but having a zombie Scout from lack of sleep does no one any good.

Other planning considerations may fall under what the team already has in the team SOP. Examples are immediate action drills, actions on contact, and communication procedures, and non-standard hand and arm signals. Always have contingency plans if a team mate becomes separated and rehearse these before you LD.

OP Security

Scouts are extremely vulnerable in an OP; their best self-defense is not to be seen, heard, or otherwise located by the enemy. They employ active and passive measures to protect themselves from enemy detection and direct and indirect fires.

The first step is to locate the OP in a covered and concealed position to reduce the chance of being seen by the enemy. The scouts add camouflage to the position to enhance natural concealment. If they have enough time and the situation allows, they dig in the position and add overhead cover to increase survivability against enemy fires. The scouts enforce strict light and noise discipline and reduce activity in and around the OP to essential movement only.

Active patrolling around and between OPs can also enhance security, but movement draws attention so as with all things METT-TC applies. Patrols give scouts the ability to observe areas that cannot be observed from the OPs and to clear the area around the OP of enemy elements. They execute security patrols as soon after occupation of the position as possible to discover enemy elements that might have observed the occupation. The patrol reconnoiters favorable observation positions that might be occupied by the enemy. Route selection is critical when organizing these patrols because the scouts must assume that the OP position is under observation.

Position Considerations. Whether a Scout team is in a position for a few minutes or a few days, the basic considerations in choosing a type of position remain the same. For defensive oriented OPs you will have additional time, and under ideal conditions these are less likely to be under enemy observation while being established. For fixed locations such as our neighborhoods you can apply significantly more resources and construction time compared to the recon or offensive oriented OPs that we will occupy for shorter duration missions. The same general principles for any OP will still apply, the degree of preparation or construction comes down to time (both occupation duration and prep time), resources, and likelihood of enemy contact.

OP Construction

After the Scout team leader makes final adjustments to the position, he ensures it is concealed and still meets the mission requirements (eg it can effectively observe the assigned area).

Enemy patrols in the area may be close enough to the position to hear any noises that may accidentally be made during any site improvements or construction. The team also considers the enemy's night vision and detection capabilities when balancing the activity required for improvements and the risk of compromise.

Covered positions provide protection from enemy fires; hide site dispersion to the rear of the OP further reduces the effects of these fires.

Construction Considerations for Subsurface OPs

Type of terrain and soil. Digging can be very difficult in hard soil or in fine, loose sand. The team should take advantage of what the terrain offers (gullies, holes, hollow tree stumps, and so forth). Just don't let this drive you to a position that is vulnerable to compromise.

The Amount of time to be occupied. If the team's mission requires it to be in position for an extended time (up to 72 hours), the team constructs a position that provides more survivability (balance the OP improvement activities with the enemy situation and likelihood of compromise). This allows the team to operate more effectively for a longer time. Time also applies to the time required for construction. The time required to build a position must be considered, especially during mission planning.

Personnel and equipment needed for construction. The team plans for the use of any extra equipment needed for construction (bow saws, picks, axes, and so forth when emplacing a defensive oriented OP). Small handheld pruning shears are a great tool to have on the OP for selectively removing branches that impede line of sight (be very cautious in their use and stash green vegetation that can wilt/quickly change color). Coordination is made if the position requires more personnel to build it or a security element to secure the area during construction. For OPs emplaced during recon missions the team is not out to build a complex bunker system, just enough to get them by for a day or two. Scouts chopping with axes and digging extensively will get the enemy's attention, so don't plan on doing this. An entrenching tool used judiciously, small pruners, and a folding saw are the tools of the trade for positions that are established within OP range of a recon objective.

OP Communications

An OP must have the means to report what they see as quickly and clearly as possible. The communications imperatives you learned earlier in CM-1 still apply; there is a balance between the urgency of the report and the risks of radio transmissions and communication detection. Wire comms between OP (or multiple OPs) back to the squad or platoon or a fixed site are more secure, but the weight and bulk penalty of these wire systems are too much for recon mission OPs and will serve you best for defensive or fixed sites. The scouts occupying the defensive OP use wire, radio, or both as their primary means of comms but wire is preferred for the defense / fixed site because it is more secure and not vulnerable to enemy direction-finding equipment. Wire is also the best way for the scouts in the OP to communicate with their squad leader or an entry

107

control point (ECP) located behind the OP. The checkpoint or defensive position cell in turn relays reports to the platoon or community command post (CP) for processing.

If they anticipate being in a position for a long period of time, scouts should construct a directional antenna to further reduce their vulnerability to enemy jamming or direction-finding. This is done at the comms site away from the OP itself, METT-TC will determine where comms sites are and if/when additional expedient antennas are emplaced. The scouts in all OPs should always carry radios as a means of communication, even if they are using wire or another means to pass information.

OP Status

Once the senior Scout on the position / Scout team leader is at the OP he will report status to his leadership (if the team is not on a self-directed mission). He will report the OP is SET when the OP is secure and can observe the assigned NAI, TRP, and/or Avenue of Approach (AoA). Remember the FM radio risks, this would be done from the comms site away from the OP. Depending on your SOP (you may always have establishment reports followed by the current slant (combat power or number of systems by SOP)) the message may sound like this:

"BLACK SIX THIS IS RED TWO-SEVEN, SET 1, SLANT 4, CONTINUING MISSION, OVER"

What the heck does that even mean? Using the radio procedures, you know it is in a standard "you this is me" format, so the reporting Scout's callsign (in this example) is RED 27. His team is at OP1 and the OP is set (the conditions we listed earlier are in place), he has 4 fully mission capable Scouts including himself, and the team is continuing the mission as planned.

A quick COMSEC/OPSEC learning point, we want to be as clear but as obscure with our uncoded messages as possible. If you are transmitting in the clear (eg without encryption, either digital or OTP codes) be sure you don't associate terms with friendly graphic control measures. Graphic control measures are the symbols and names we use to designate locations or actions, eg OP1, PHASE LINE BAMA, OBJ HAMMER etc. Make it as difficult as you can for an unauthorized listener to associate or figure out what a reference is. We don't want to say "OP1 is set" or "crossing Phase Line BAMA", we only refer to the number or name. We would say "SET 1," or "crossing BAMA" when transmitting in the clear. Your unit will know that "1" is an OP, but someone eavesdropping will not. It doesn't equate to secure comms by any stretch of the imagination, but every little bit helps...or hurts if done improperly.

Improving the position

Once the team leader has set the OP and assigned the scouts their sectors of observation, the scouts improve the position. The squad or patrol leader prepares a sector sketch. This sketch is similar to a fighting position sketch but with some differences. At a minimum, the sketch will include a rough sketch of key and significant terrain; the location of the OP; the location of the hide position; the location of adjacent observation positions; alternate positions (hide, fighting, observation); routes to the OP and any fighting positions (if present); sectors of observation; preplanned artillery targets (if used); TRPs for direct fire; and prepared spot reports based on trigger lines and projected locations where the enemy will first be seen.

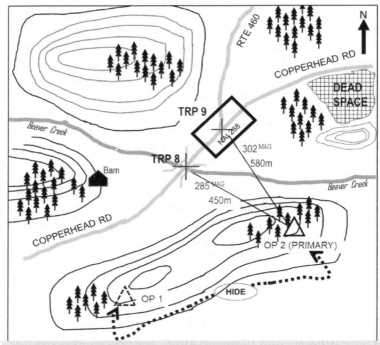

Simplified sector sketch of OPs (primary and templated alternate positions). There are no wrong answers for your sketch, capture any information you deem necessary. Anything that would help another Scout understand the plan and relationship of the team and the terrain.

As part of the priorities of work and improvements scouts manning the OP site may begin digging in to provide protection from indirect and direct fires (METT-TC dependent, every situation will be different). They also camouflage the position, install wire communications equipment (if used) and directional antennas for FM communications, and may emplace hasty obstacles and warning devices for local protection (traps, tripwires etc).

If the OP is planned to be more robust or longer term, after the OP is set the team will execute priorities of work to get it ESTABLISHED (the next status in the progression). This

110

is an OP where Scouts have hide/fighting positions, range cards/sector sketches are complete, TRPs are coordinated with other OPs (if there are any others), positions are camouflaged, and the OP is more defendable. Battle drills for viable forms of contact should be planned and verbally rehearsed. OP teams should work towards transforming a SET OP to an ESTABLISHED OP, the patrol leader should dictate a time for the OP to be established after set, based off your team SOP. Once established the same type of message is relayed to your headquarters/parent unit just as before.

Find a safe way to communicate when your team has met requirements such as setting the OP. Balancing the communications risk is an important task for leaders with the support of the RTOs.

Chapter 3
Scouting at Night (Introductory Overview)

Own the night. This is not just a mantra; night is prime time for our operations. We are including this as a **brief introductory** chapter on night fighting to get you thinking about training for night movement, operations and shifting your mindset from a daytime focus.

Things change in the darkness, both in the physical and psychological realms. Most of us on the team prefer being out at night. We become more focused; everyone is fixated on the job. The environmental noise settles down as the woods (and even the desert) settle down for the night. Predators start to move about and begin to hunt, the air cools and typically the wind dies down compared to daytime to add to the silence. Enemy sentries can be less alert, and troops fall asleep. It is the best time for us to be out.

Most of the population has not trained extensively or even done shift work for a job outdoors during the night, much less done so without a white light source. Being able to move at night without running into things or just staying awake on a patrol is not the end goal. We must be proficient at night to leverage the advantages of darkness against a threat. Nighttime affords the guerilla force not only the advantage of stealth, but also carries a distinct psychological edge. Being scared of things in the dark isn't just for children, we can instill that fear in a threat as well.

Although operating at night has significant advantages, we are all aware it also has challenges associated with it. Human eyes do not work as well as daylight, it is more difficult to control formations, detecting and engaging threats is different and can be more difficult than during daylight hours. There is one standout exception to this, direct fire engagements at night under thermals are incredibly easy. Recommend keeping this in mind as you choose routes and negotiate terrain at night; just because you have difficulty seeing and have reduced range under light amplifying NV don't assume you aren't in someone's thermal sight picture. Plan your routes accordingly.

Just staying oriented and keeping your position in formation is tough at night (old school cat eyes are your friend, if employed correctly they will not be a detriment to light discipline). Time/distance relationships change at night, tasks will take longer to accomplish, and detection / engagement ranges will shorten. The effects of adverse weather become more pronounced.

See first, act first. No different than daytime, the side that sees the other first has the advantage; this advantage can oftentimes be a decisive one. Having a well trained and experienced Point Man, NV systems available for all team members, and leadership who understands lighting conditions and maximizing capabilities will be the edge that provides the win. Depending on lighting you may mix formations with some using passive NV and some not. You might be thinking if you have the NV device capability why wouldn't you *always* use it during a movement? There are times when ambient lighting conditions provide enough light to allow individuals with good natural night vision to be more effective without it. Yes, they should have it available (flipped up on their helmet) if those conditions change or if contact is made. Remember your young Scouts will have the best natural night vision, so consider that when weighing options. Always keep in mind there are no absolutes or "school solutions" for a lot of this. Train under various lighting conditions and see what works for you.

Light Discipline and breaking the light habit. Many of our inexperienced team members tend to rely on using visible light, training them out of this is necessary. Most of it comes from not understanding how dark adaptation works or how far a small or even a red lens light can be seen outdoors. Conduct demonstrations during training to show them what various lights look like with natural adapted vision and then under nods. Examples of close and long distance white light, lighter flame, campfires, stoves, red lens flashlight, IR lasers, and IR illuminators will go a long way to show them the real risk to the unit.

There are countless lighting conditions and combinations that are present in an environment, but they fall into two distinct large categories. There are multiple definitions of ambient light, for the ease of our discussion we will roll ambient into one large chunk. Each will have its own challenges for a unit working in the dark. The "so what?" of this is it allows you to plan and adjust your techniques and tools you will use for the situation. If there is a significant amount of ambient light (for example the typical neighborhood street lights) you may choose to a monocular so you can read and use shadows more easily, or even opt to have some team members go without NV altogether. There are no canned solutions, it is a thinking person's game. Understanding variables and knowing how to adjust to them is the way; this is especially true at night.

Ambient (either natural or artificial) light. Ambient light is existing light we did not bring to the environment. Also known as available light, it is any light source that you haven't set up or activated yourself. This includes natural light or pre-existing lighting built in and around a location, a structure or street. Examples are sunlight, moonlight, streetlamps, facility floodlights, or even the existing artificial lighting that is on inside a building.

Directed artificial light (Active). Searchlights, spotlights, flashlights, or headlights on a vehicle are all examples of this. Weapon mounted lights and handheld flashlights are in this category as well. Visible directed artificial light in any form (any color or spectrum) is always active; we must assume it can always be detected by an opponent. IR lights are also included in the active category - and we must always assume any threat to have a passive NV capability.

Although they are not visible to the human eye, any IR laser or illuminator is an active source of light. Always assume the enemy can see your lasers, illuminators, and IR strobes/markers.

Twilight. Twilight induces a false sense of security, and we must be extremely cautious. The enemy is also prone to carelessness and more likely to expose himself at twilight. During twilight, scouts should be alert to OP locations for future reference. Non-illuminated optic reticles are generally still visible and capable of accurate fire at BMNT and up to EENT if the background factors are favorable. Always be sure to adjust illuminated reticles / red dots up or down during these transitional periods as part of your Pre Combat Checks (PCC).

BMNT - Begin Morning Nautical Twilight is the time of morning when in good conditions and in the absence of other illumination, enough light is available to identify the general outlines of ground objects and conduct limited military operations. Light intensification devices are still effective and may have enhanced capabilities. For iron sights this is "first shooting light". It is just enough illumination with the naked eye to make out shapes. Positive ID is not possible under these conditions.

BMNT occurs before sunrise and can be affected by weather or smoke and is influenced by existing snow cover. Daylight movement planning can be based on BMNT, the flip side is this is when unknown/adversarial individuals without the aid of night vision can start effectively maneuvering. BMNT is also the time that the woods "wake up". This is not the time to get up, stretch and scratch yourself, you should be up and ready to fight prior to BMNT (see various REDCON status in CM-1). Ground animals will start to move about, and birds will begin chirping. Presence or absence of these animal sounds can be an indication of human or predator movement. The US Naval Observatory website has light data tables that you can select by date that will indicate when BMNT occurs, your intelligence specialist (your BICC in the heavy squad). *BMCT/EECT – Begin Morning Civil Twilight/End Evening Civil Twilight.* Begin Morning Civil twilight is the brightest of the twilight phases in the morning since it is just before official sunrise. Generically both these twilights can be referred to as dawn or dusk, but most of us have our own ill-defined definition (and there are actually three official "dawns" and three "dusks" each day) so we will leave those out of our vocabulary for now. The sun is just below the horizon and getting brighter (BMCT) or just below it and getting darker (EECT). There is usually enough natural light to carry out most tasks without artificial light. BMCT ends at sunrise; in the evening EECT begins after sunset. Think of when streetlights come on in most neighborhoods, that is roughly around EECT. Only the brightest stars and planets can be observed with the naked eye during these phases.

EENT - End Evening Nautical Twilight. EENT is the final fading of the light after the sun disappears below the horizon. Night operations should be planned for after EENT (couple this with moon and illumination data). EENT is the instant of last available daylight for the unaided visual control of ground operations (illumination from moonlight notwithstanding).

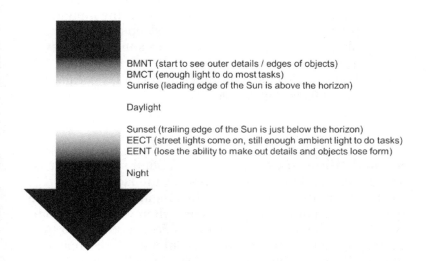

BMNT (start to see outer details / edges of objects)
BMCT (enough light to do most tasks)
Sunrise (leading edge of the Sun is above the horizon)

Daylight

Sunset (trailing edge of the Sun is just below the horizon)
EECT (street lights come on, still enough ambient light to do tasks)
EENT (lose the ability to make out details and objects lose form)

Night

117

Natural Night Vision. We must be aware of the constraints your eyes place upon you at night. Roughly 80 percent of your sensory input comes through vision, learning how to work around the negative effects of darkness takes time and training.

Some of these constraints we must understand:

- Your ability to see crisp and clear images (your visual acuity) is reduced and under certain conditions, you cannot distinguish one color from another.
- Your depth perception is reduced (and no, dual tube NV does not increase the user's depth perception).
- You have "night blind spot," which makes it difficult to see objects at certain distances.
- Lights cause the loss of dark adaptation. This includes red lens flashlights, the screens of thermal or NV systems, and of course white light.
- Your eyes may seem to play tricks on you, just like when we were kids you will start to see things as the reduced visual acuity combines with the human psyche especially when we are sleep deprived. Shapes can appear to move or be something they are not.
- You will also have slower reaction times because of the reduced lighting levels.

Normal Blind Spots. The "normal blind spot" is always present, day and night. It is caused by the lack of light receptors where the optic nerve inserts into the back of the eye. The "normal blind spot" occurs when you use just one eye. When you close the other eye, objects about 12 to 15 degrees away from where you are looking will disappear. When you uncover your eye, the objects will reappear.

Night Blind Spots and Viewing Techniques. When you stare at an object at night with the naked eye under low levels of illumination, it can seem to disappear or fade away. This is a result of the night blind spot. It affects both eyes at the same time and occurs when using the central vision of both eyes. Consequently, even large objects are missed as the distances increase. If you are looking directly at something at night, you may miss it because of the night blind spot.

In order to avoid this night blind spot with the unaided eye, look to all sides of objects you are trying to find or follow. This is referred to as off center vision. *Do not stare.* It is an individual training component to learn not to stare or strain when your attention is on an object at night. This is the only way to maximize your unaided night vision.

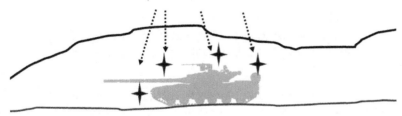

Look slightly away from the object so the image is formed on the rod region of the eye (your natural night vision). Look offset at the ✛ not directly at the tank

Off Center vision scanning will allow you to still see some objects at night with the unaided eye. Just don't revert back to direct vision out of habit, the target will literally "disappear"

A good technique for peripheral viewing is called "diamond viewing." Diamond viewing means that you move your eyes just slightly, a few degrees, in a diamond pattern around the object you wish to see. You do not have to move your head-use your peripheral vision, just slight eye movement off the target will do the job.

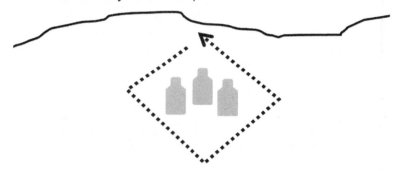

Look in a diamond pattern around the outer edge; not directly at the troops

Diamond viewing scanning will keep the eye moving and prevents the blind spot target "disappearance".

Darkness not only makes objects difficult to see but also changes their appearance, distorts size, and blots out details. A tree visible against the night sky appears smaller than in the daytime because the twigs at the end of branches cannot be seen. A Scout must train to identify objects by block outlines at night and cannot rely on details visible in daylight. Binoculars enlarge objects or parts of objects otherwise too small to be seen and help identify objects already spotted. Night observation devices increase night visibility and should be used when the situation requires (odds are this will be most times).

An object once found must stay found. If you spot something of interest (using natural vision) it is important to not lose sight of it. The tendency will be to revert to the daylight vision and look directly at it. Do not do this. When we "lose" an object at night it is very difficult to reacquire it. Using the offset vision technique or switching to an NV system can keep you in visual contact with the object. This is especially true if the target is moving away (increasing in range).

Illusion (Apparent Movement of Light). The illusion of movement, which a static light exhibits when stared at in the dark, is related to the loss of surrounding visual references that normally serve to stabilize visual perceptions. Consequently, very small eye movements are perceived by the brain as movement of the light. Lay out under the stars for a while and you will see this in action, a particular star will seem to move if you focus on it too long. Especially if it is relatively brighter and stands out compared to the night sky. This same phenomenon is what we are guarding against by using eye movement and scan patterns. Use large movements and scan to control illusions. Try to find another light and shift your gaze back and forth between the two.

Dark Adaptation

For your visual system to work efficiently at night, you need to dark adapt. Dark adaptation is the process by which the human body increases the eyes' sensitivity to low levels of light. During the first 30 minutes in the dark, eye sensitivity increases about 10,000 times, but not much more after that. It takes the rod cells in the human eye about 30 minutes to produce enough visual purple (the red or purple pigment in the retina that is sensitive to dim light) to enable the eye to distinguish objects in dim light; and about 45 minutes to fully dark-adapt. It takes longer to dark adapt than many people think, but only a moment of bright light to undo it.

People will dark adapt at varying rates. Older individuals, smokers, or those who are out of physical shape will take longer to dark adapt or see things under low light conditions.

Dark adaptation is affected by exposure to bright light such as matches, flashlights, flares, or vehicle headlights. Full recovery from these exposures can take up to 45 minutes.

Color perception decreases at night. You may be able to distinguish light and dark colors depending on the intensity of reflected light. Visual sharpness is also reduced. Since visual sharpness at night is one seventh of what it is during the day, individuals can see only large, bulky objects. This means that object identification at night is based on generalized contours and outlines. Depth perception is also affected negatively.

Stages of Adaptation. There are three stages of dark adaptation that help to explain how the eye works at night.

Daylight Vision. The first stage is daylight vision, which occurs under maximum lighting conditions such as when the sun is shining or in a well-lit room. Under these conditions, both your central and peripheral vision are used, which provides your best visual acuity-20/10, 20/15, and 20/20 vision. You also have your best color vision-colors look most vivid under daylight conditions. You also have your quickest reaction time.

Twilight Vision. The next stage of adaptation is twilight vision. Twilight vision occurs during many military night operations. It occurs at BMNT/EENT, and down to full moonlight. It also occurs when there is artificial illumination and when snow is on the ground at night. It can also occur in the daytime when under several layers of jungle or tree canopy that can create lower lighting conditions.

Because of the lower light levels at BMNT, between EECT and EENT, and full moon conditions, your visual acuity can be as low as 20/100. In fact, the best visual acuity you can hope to obtain under twilight conditions is between 20/50 and 20/100. For all the non-eye doctors out there (I had to look it up as well) it is tied to distance. 20/100 vision just means you have to be 20 feet away from the object to see the same details as 20/20 vision eyeball looking at the same object from 100 feet away.

Humans also have poorer color vision in twilight conditions. You can still see colors, but they won't be as vivid. Your chosen camo pattern and colors may become more or less effective depending on conditions and the colors you choose.

Night Vision. The third and final vision category is night vision (the natural type, not the electronically enhanced type). Also called scotopic vision, it is your natural unaided ability to see in the dark. Night vision occurs under starlight, as well as on moonless and cloudy nights when there are no stars or cultural lighting. Remember there is a "night blind spot" as discussed earlier. In a dark setting, your eyes like to gather as much light as possible. They do this by opening the pupils wide and allowing your eyes to catch as many rough outlines and shapes as they can. In a brighter setting your pupils shrink back down, since they have all the light they need to see comfortably.

Under night conditions, everyone has poor visual acuity-from 20/200 to 20/400 and possibly much worse. You can recognize silhouettes, but not the details of the objects. The younger the Scout the better the natural night vision since human night vision peaks in the teenage years. Yay youth.

Under night vision conditions we cannot see colors, only various shades of gray can be seen. With natural night vision, the longer wavelengths of light, such as the reds and oranges, are hard to see and will appear dark. Unless a dark color is bordered by two lighter colors, it becomes totally invisible. Keep this in mind as you assess your camouflage selection. Reds will be almost invisible at night. On the other hand, greens and blues will appear brighter, although you may not be able to determine their color.

Protecting (Before Mission). It is very important to protect your eyes before night operations so you can dark-adapt in an efficient manner.

Don't smoke before nighttime operations. Not smoking four to six hours before night operations will aid in dark adaptation. None of us should be smoking at any time as it is, it is one of the habits that a Citizen should avoid or break immediately.

If outdoors wear sunglasses in the last hour before sunset. Doing so can speed the dark adaptation process once the sun goes down. Without sunglasses it will take longer to dark-adapt. And it sounds kind of funny, but I have seen units (good units) even blindfold themselves for a half hour or so before leaving the secure area to go out on a mission. Also makes for some nice quiet settle down time for the dudes to get their minds right before heading out.

Use dim white lighting in buildings / facilities or dim red lighting before night operations.

Protecting (During Mission). Once you are dark-adapted it is critical to maintain that dark adaptation. Nothing will enrage a Scout more than an inexperienced teammate using a light (red or otherwise) around them. New/inexperienced folks will tend toward the use of light vs feeling around for items in a ruck or to adjust a piece of gear in the patrol base. Experienced dudes understand just how long it takes to regain that dark adaptation and they will relentlessly guard it. Looking through any NV device will negatively affect your dark adaptation; even though it is night vision it is still a bright light source going into the eye. If a fighter adapts to the dark before donning the goggles, he generally gains full dark adaptation under most conditions within two minutes when they are removed *(Optical Filter Effects on Night Vision Goggle Acuity and Preservation of Dark Adaptation; Roger S. Thomas , Steve T. Wright , Patrick J. Clark , William T. Thompson , and John M. Gooch, August 2009).*

Minimize your use of unnecessary lighting (including red) to maintain your dark adaptation during operations at night.

Close one eye before being flashed by flares and other bright lights (such as passing headlights) to preserve your dark adaptation. If you are leaving a secure area in the dark ensure your defensive plan accounts for patrols leaving at night. Launching a patrol through a brightly lit entry control point or an area with a lot of ambient light should be avoided, but as always we don't want to set patterns or use the same gates or gaps every time we go out.

You don't need the gain maxed out on your NV systems to see. Turning the gain down on your system will not prevent natural night vision loss, but it can make the adaptation process a bit faster if it is dimmed down. This will also aid in the light spill or splash from the rear of your NV unit especially if you don't have the eyecups attached to the units.

Night Vision Devices

There are three devices available to dismounted Scouts that will help increase his effectiveness at night. Night Observation Devices (NODs), aiming lasers, and thermal viewers or weapon sights. Each provides the dismounted Scout with different views of the infrared (IR) spectrum. Your team must understand what limitations and advantages each piece of equipment has so that they can determine when to employ each device. We won't dig into specifications or numbers, just a short discussion of big picture NV components to build some understanding.

Electromagnetic (Light) Spectrum. The electromagnetic spectrum is simply energy (light). Within this spectrum of energy or light you can find x-rays, gamma rays, radio waves, cosmic rays, and ultra violet rays, to name a few. Also within this spectrum of light is visible light, visible light being what we are able to see with the naked eye. Just beyond red visible light is IR light, meaning just beyond. IR light is broken down into three different ranges: near IR, middle IR, and far IR. This is important for the Scout to know because it will give him an understanding of why some night devices cannot be used in conjunction with other night devices.

There are two different types of devices in the IR range. The first one is image intensifiers (I^2), which rely on ambient light and energy in the near IR range emitted from light sources such as moonlight or starlight. Image intensifiers include the PVS-14 and dual tube night vision. There are also devices that emit near IR energy in a collimated beam, which are used as laser aiming devices such as the PEQ, BE Meyers MAWL, DBAL, and countless other models. Since the image intensifiers and aiming lasers work within the same range of near IR energy they can work in conjunction with each other. Some units may run afoul of one another, there are indeed tube models that can have issues with some IR laser emitters. Make sure you identify any incompatibilities on your team beforehand. And be careful using your tubes around lasers, more than a few NV units have burned in laser spots.

With the proliferation of light amplifying NV systems we must assume any threat will have them (we discussed this earlier in this manual). Active IR emission is high risk, we have seen the IR laser fall in importance as this risk has been realized. Passive aiming is where we need to focus our energy (no pun intended).

The second device that uses IR light is the thermal sight. These devices until very recently were very bulky, heavy and not very practical for the dismounted Scout due to being power intensive. Fortunately for us the market has numerous thermal devices that are purpose built for the dismounted individual. The hunting community (especially feral hog hunters) have been the driving force for generating the current family of lightweight, low power consumption thermal optics for us. These can be mounted on weapons, handheld, or mounted on a helmet. Thermal weapons sights and viewers operate within the middle/far IR range. They can detect IR light emitted from friction, combustion, or from objects that are radiating natural thermal energy. Since thermal devices operate within the middle/far IR range they cannot be used in conjunction with image intensifiers or other I² devices at this time. They also cannot see through glass, a window pane or windshield is impenetrable by current thermal technology. Glass will appear as if it is a blank mirror when observed through a thermal.

Image Intensifiers (I²) Device Types. As the name implies, image intensification devices are designed to amplify light. When light enters the image intensifier tube, the light releases electrons, which the tube accelerates repeatedly until the light is much brighter. There are three general categories we may choose, the monocular (such as the PVS-14), the bi-ocular (the obsolete AN/PVS-7B...don't recommend as they combine the worst of both options), or the binocular (dual tube) goggles. The PVS14 and duals are available in green or white phosphor (details of general NV selection requirements are discussed in depth inside the

CM-1). Ok, there *is* a fourth category with the GPNVG (pano), but at $40k+ per unit they may be past the point of expenditure justification for most Citizens.

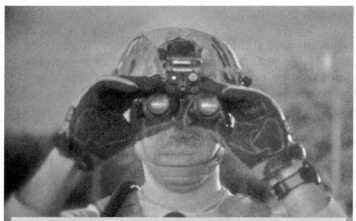

Don't think for a minute that you must use dual tubes to be effective. A good PVS14 unit is the typical entry point for new NV users.

Bump or Ballistic? The Scout has plenty of options for NV mounting systems, the big two decisions if using a helmet option are between a bump or ballistic. Our position is if you are putting up with the helmet then you should go ahead and get some ballistic protection out of it. The weight of modern helmets has come down significantly. While a bump will always be lighter it won't be lighter by much if you choose a lightweight ballistic helmet. Quick note on these, do NOT buy a cheap ballistic helmet from overseas. Stick with a known, reputable manufacturer. Some of the manufacturers in the good to go category are OpsCore, Team Wendy, Crye, and MTEK just to name a few. Bumps are cooler and lighter, but if you are going to carry the volume and weight of the helmet you might as well get as much capability out of it as possible.

Chapter 4
Mission Planning and Preparation

General Reconnaissance Considerations. Adapting reconnaissance fundamentals for Citizen patrols puts us on solid doctrinal ground since many of our missions will most likely be (or start off as) recon in nature. It also lends itself to the application of many of the guerilla tactics. The guerilla force must be stealthy, averse to making direct fire contact unless there is an overwhelming and near immediate chance of success and be able to disappear into the terrain after any enemy engagement. The stealth and aversion to contact imperatives of the guerilla force are well supported by the requirements of recon patrols. These principles are at the heart of recon and will facilitate transitioning to limited ambushes or raids, sabotage, and interdiction of enemy support troops through ambushes and raids. This does not mean that our guerilla / Citizen type organizations do not conduct other types of missions; this recon-centric approach simply makes the most sense to use as the starting point for building proficiency for our anticipated role.

Recon vs Surveillance. Surveillance is the systematic observation of areas, places, persons, or things by visual, aural, electronic, photographic, or other means. Instead of focusing on one specific piece of required information, reconnaissance will provide you with a broader understanding of the impacts of terrain, weather, and enemy that assists planning or actions. This is not to be misunderstood as it being open ended effort; recon is *always* focused with the purpose to answer information requirements in the form of Priority Information Requirements (PIR) and the commander's (leader's) reconnaissance guidance. Surveillance is more persistent and tends to be more passive than reconnaissance.

Reconnaissance (Recon) is a mission undertaken to obtain information about the activities and resources of an enemy or adversary, or to gather data about the terrain (OAKOC analysis) or other characteristics of an area. It is gathering information from the field in areas outside the control of friendly forces and entails sending scouts or sensors of some kind into enemy territory to gather information.

Reconnaissance identifies terrain characteristics, enemy and friendly obstacles to movement, the disposition of enemy forces and the civilian population. There may be friendly command posts where this information is processed and fused together as intelligence (packaged into a usable and understandable form).

Reconnaissance prior to unit movements and occupation of safe haven or assembly areas is critical to protecting friendly forces and preserving combat power. We cannot afford to have our main units or our protected members get ambushed by a threat we should have discovered.

Reconnaissance Fundamentals. Six fundamentals are common to all successful reconnaissance operations. Patrol leaders must ensure that their plans adhere to these fundamentals during the reconnaissance.

Maintain tempo and focus. As the leader plans and executes the unit's reconnaissance missions, he must ensure that the unit keeps its focus on the reconnaissance objective(s) and maintains the operational tempo of the mission. A patrol that loses either focus or tempo will quickly lose its combat effectiveness.

Orient on the reconnaissance objective. The guerilla force in a scout role must use a scheme of maneuver that is focused on a specific objective or set of objectives. These may be a terrain feature, an area, or an enemy force; it may be designated by an area of interest (the NAIs we described earlier), checkpoint, or objective. The unit must maintain its orientation toward the objective, regardless of what it encounters, until the mission is complete. It is critical that the patrol leader completely understand the mission's focus before he begins the planning process.

Report all information rapidly and accurately. Leaders base their decisions and plans on the information that scouts find and report during reconnaissance. Information loses value over time. Scouts must report all information exactly as they see it and as fast as possible and do it without emotion. They must never assume, distort, or exaggerate; inaccurate information is dangerous (see CM-1 for SALUTE and SALT report discussion). Timely reporting will always be an issue for the guerilla force as it will likely require use of a detectable means (radio) which presents a set of risks and challenges.

Retain freedom to maneuver. Guerilla squads must be able to maneuver on the battlefield. If the enemy fixes them, they must free themselves; otherwise, they can no longer accomplish their mission. The guerilla force must remain stealthy and be unattainable to the enemy. When contact is made, the patrol leader must quickly develop the situation at the lowest possible level, retain the initiative, the ability to continue the mission, and the ability to maneuver his other elements to not be decisively engaged.

Gain and maintain enemy contact. Seek visual contact with the enemy on favorable terms **(we see them, but they do not see us).** Recon teams employ sound tactical movement, effective target acquisition methods, and appropriate actions on contact to see the enemy first and retain the initiative. Once you find the enemy, your patrol will maintain contact using all available means (sensors, sound, and visual) until directed/ordered to do otherwise or as required by their specific instructions.

Develop the situation rapidly. When guerilla fighters run into an enemy force or an obstacle, they must quickly determine what they are up against. If it is the enemy, they determine his size, composition, and activity and locate the flanks of the enemy force. They find any barriers or obstacles surrounding the enemy position and determine whether any other enemy forces can support the position. If you encounter an obstacle, find and mark a bypass per your unit SOP and collect detailed data to send to the command post / intelligence fusion cell. This all must be done quickly with a minimum of guidance from higher and without detection. Time and stealth are the guerilla scout's most precious resources.

Planning and Operational Considerations

You and your group cannot only fight from SOPs, you must analyze and plan every mission independently. Operations are planned against a task and purpose; what you are doing and why you are doing it. SOPs, battle drills and TTPs will augment and inform unit actions that are not mission specific, however they cannot be relied on solely to execute a mission. The patrol leader must understand his mission and be able to convey it to his unit. He develops this knowledge by conducting mission analysis to identify all specified and implied tasks and understand the enemy, terrain, and the commander's intent for any given mission.

Mission type orders and Commanders Intent. *Mission Type Orders* are not a specific type, they describe the "style" or characteristic of permissiveness in that they are designed to enable disciplined initiative. Mission type orders empower subordinate leaders. In the absence of further orders and under changing conditions a subordinate leader can apply judgment and still accomplish the goal of the mission even if he must improvise a solution. Applying this characteristic when issuing orders will build trust. As the conditions change so long as the leaders understand the intent of a mission they have the latitude to adjust the "how" to accomplish the "why" from a mission. Clear commander's guidance with a well-articulated intent empowers the Scout to think like the commander and take the same actions as that he would if he were on your patrol.

Patrol leaders must:

Understand Mission and Intent. At a minimum, the patrol leader understands the focus of the mission *even if it is a self directed mission* (terrain-, enemy-, or civilian oriented, or a combination), the tempo of the operation, and his engagement criteria. He also develops the facts and assumptions related to his mission using the factors of METT-TC.

Understand how to use Intelligence. The patrol leader must understand the IPB process (in an applicable form according to his capabilities as we discussed earlier).

Manage Time Wisely. The patrol leader makes efficient use of the time available for planning, preparation, and issuing the order. The patrol leader can't be a time thief, giving team leaders and team members more time than we take during mission preparation is the mark of a mature leader. You must ensure your subordinate leaders have sufficient time to conduct their own troop-leading procedures. Refer to the discussion of reverse planning and timeline development later in this chapter.

Issue effective orders. The patrol leader must be able to issue a clear operation order (OPORD) that conveys the nature of the mission to his subordinates. He can issue these orders orally, digitally, or using a combination of these. Most likely the orders for our purposes will be oral and in person, updates or FRAGOs may go out via FM however the risk of detection must be mitigated (see the comms chapter in CM-1).

Conduct focused rehearsals. The patrol leader must be proficient in conducting rehearsals. At a minimum, he

133

conducts rehearsals of major events in the mission, actions on the objective, contact/battle drills, and casualty evacuation (CASEVAC).

Conduct precombat checks and inspections. The patrol conducts, at a minimum, precombat checks (PCC) and if feasible, precombat inspections (PCI) before the mission begins to ensure fighters are prepared and have confidence in their equipment.

Be an expert at reading and using terrain. Urban or rural, being able to see the terrain and how the fight will unfold is critical. Navigating is a basic skill, but visualizing how the enemy and friendly unit will use the terrain and environment is the graduate level work a patrol leader must understand fully. Leveraging advantages of the terrain, finding and exploiting enemy weak points, and keeping his fighters out of unneeded danger are absolute imperatives for a long-term fight. It takes years of experience to become truly proficient at this, selecting mature leaders who have experience mixed with intuition and hard skills is recommended.

Own the night. The patrol leader in a Citizen unit must not simply be comfortable moving at night, he must be an expert at night fighting. Hours of darkness hold significant advantages for the patrol, both by concealing movement and operating while there is less activity among the local population. The patrol leader must understand enemy sensor capabilities (NV and thermal) and how to counter them. The guerilla force will need every advantage during missions, leveraging those provided by darkness is mandatory.

LD their unit in good order. The key to success is ensuring that the patrol is prepared to move by the time specified in the order with functioning weapons and equipment. All personnel must be able to explain the unit's mission (during rehearsals and PCIs), the higher commander's intent, the mission, and their specified tasks and duties to support the mission. No plan survives first contact, but stepping off on a mission with a confident, well organized, well-rehearsed unit is critical. If you are messed up at LD you will struggle to recover during execution.

> *No plan ever survives first contact. Regardless of this fact we must still deliberately plan in detail and cross the LD in good order...or we will never recover.*
> *- LTC J. Feeley*

The IPB Process (Intelligence Preparation of the Battlefield). Intelligence drives operations. *Using the IPB process keeps us from just "playing Army"* and prevents us from launching a patrol with nothing more than a video game type mission. Only by driving missions with intelligence will you maintain focus (and legitimacy) for your team. Conducting un-purposed patrols or going out just for the sake of going out will waste time, resources, and even friendly lives. IPB is the systematic process of analyzing and visualizing a geographic area for a mission (current or anticipated). This is graduate level work typically not done at the squad/heavy squad level, but as we discussed earlier all of our small unit leaders will be required to perform planning tasks at levels well above their organizational position. You may be fortunate to have staff functions supported at small group command posts, but if these are not present these critical planning and intel functions must still be performed in some form. IPB has elements that are familiar to you from CM-1 as it shares many of the components of the METT-TC analysis discussed in that manual. Starting with a deliberate and constantly updated METT-TC analysis and a focused OAKOC study of your anticipated terrain is a good way to begin this process. We will not dive deep into IPB here, for now just understand why and how it fits into mission planning.

As a small independent unit, the intelligence assessments you do prior to execution will define your mission and provide decision making information. This collection of information will determine when (or if) you execute a mission. The IPB process is continuous, so the mission you conduct will provide more information that will drive the next mission and so on. The process does not have an end point, it is nonstop.

Combat Orders

Combat orders are how the leader receives and transmits information from the earliest notification that an operation will occur through the final steps of execution. Warning Orders (WARNOs), Operation Orders (OPORDs), and Fragmentary Orders (FRAGOs) are critical to mission success. In a tactical situation leaders and subordinates work with combat orders daily and must know the correct format for each type of order. This allows us to have a common framework that is efficient and prevents confusion or mistakes. Leaders must also ensure that every fighter in the unit understands how to receive and respond to these various types of orders. The skills associated with generating and issuing orders are highly perishable. Take every opportunity to train your group and units in the use of combat orders with realistic practice. If you have an event scheduled, publish an order for it. Range day, FTX etc, these are a great way to practice writing and distributing orders and will get your team used to operating from those formats. Below is a quick refresher from CM-1 content before we discuss TLPs.

Warning Order (WARNO). Leaders will alert their units by using a WARNO during the planning for an operation. A WARNO is simply a "heads up" to give your team as much planning and prep time as possible. WARNOs also initiate a valuable time management tool— the parallel planning process. The leader will issue a series of warning orders to his subordinate leaders to help them prepare for new missions. The directions and guidelines in the WARNO allow subordinates to begin their own planning and preparation activities.

The content of WARNOs is based on two major variables:

(1) Information available about the upcoming operation and special instructions. The information usually comes from the higher HQ in a mature environment. Early on these missions will be self-directed. The leader wants his subordinates to take appropriate action, so he normally issues his WARNOs either as he receives additional orders from the HQ or as he completes his own analysis of the situation.

(2) In addition to alerting the unit to the upcoming operation, WARNOs allow the patrol leader to issue tactical information incrementally and, ultimately, to shorten the length of the actual OPORD. WARNOs do not have a specific format, but one technique to follow is the five paragraph OPORD format.

Operation Order. The OPORD is the five-paragraph directive issued by a leader to subordinates for the purpose of implementing the coordinated execution of an operation (doctrine will contradict itself with the name, for example the current 5-0 it is "Operation" order where the current Ranger Handbook it is an "Operations" Order. Subordinates will understand either one, so it is not a critical point to argue). When time and information are available, the leader will normally issue a complete OPORD as part of his TLP. However, after issuing a series of WARNOs, he does not need to repeat information previously covered. He can simply review previously issued information or brief the changes or earlier omissions. He then will have more time to concentrate on visualizing his concept of the fight for his subordinates. As noted in his WARNOs, the leader also may issue an execution matrix either to supplement the OPORD or as a tool to aid in the execution of the mission. The matrix order technique does not replace a written five-paragraph OPORD.

Fragmentary Order. A FRAGO is an abbreviated form of an OPORD (verbal, written, or digital) that normally follows the five-paragraph format. It is usually issued on a day-to-day basis that eliminates the need for restating information contained in a basic OPORD. It is issued after an OPORD (you have to have an existing order to "FRAGO off of") to change or modify that order. FRAGOs are normally focused on the next mission. The leader uses a FRAGO to communicate changes in the enemy or friendly situation, task subordinate elements based on changes in the situation or implement timely changes to existing orders, or provide pertinent extracts from more detailed orders until he can develop a detailed order.

Planning

The plan itself is just the result - the planning process is the critical component. Using a framework to assess the tactical problem set allows you to gain an understanding of the elements that will drive your decisions. This section describes portions of the planning process in detail and may be somewhat overwhelming. If you are just starting to learn and understand this process view this like when you first learned land navigation. It may seem complex and jumbled at first as you try and digest all the pieces, but once you are familiar with the process and have practiced it in the field it will all come together and start making sense. Just as the map was once just a collection of shapes and colors it now paints a holistic picture for you. You will come to a similar understanding of planning as you put these components together and it becomes one entity vs a random collection of information and actions. It takes time and practice, just be patient with yourself and your group as you hone this skill.

Processes described below may (and will) be in more detail than you can account for in your planning, especially in a time or personnel constrained environment. The more preparation and training you do now will help fill in the gaps if you don't have time or resources during a mission planning drill. For example, doing a full terrain analysis is not feasible in a time constrained planning cycle, but a lot of the groundwork (no pun intended) of that analysis can be done now. It is very likely that you will be somewhat familiar with the terrain in your AO, use this time to become intimately familiar with it and do the required detail work before you are forced to. It is far easier to adjust an existing body of work than start from scratch after X Hour. We won't go too deep into orders process / writing an OPORD in this manual, the takeaway from this section is learning TLPs and the process. While orders are outputs from TLPs we want to keep this fairly surface level and will address orders in detail inside future manuals.

Military Decision Making Process (MDMP)

Troop Leading Procedures (TLP) and The Army Military Decision Making Process (MDMP) both provide an approach to decision making that helps leaders analyze a situation and reach logical conclusions. Which planning method you choose will depend on the situation, the talent and availability of staff, your experience and comfort with the process, and the decision that needs to be made. MDMP goes into extreme detail and is a thorough process to reach the best possible solution (a Course of Action (COA)). Larger unit commanders with trained staff use the MDMP as their primary planning process which is more complex and time intensive than TLPs. For our purposes we will focus on TLPs since we are discussing squad and enhanced squad level planning and therefore it is most likely what you will use for planning.

Troop Leading Procedures (TLPs)

Troop-leading procedures (TLP) provide a framework for decision making during the plan and prepare phases of a mission. You will use TLP when working as independent teams or with a small group to solve tactical problems. When in a leadership position you will use subordinates to help you with the process. For example, a squad leader may use the team leaders, the RTO or USO to assist during TLPs. As we walk through learning the TLPs keep in mind that you can practice it on your own for any task that has a few moving pieces. Anything from taking the family on a vacation, a camping trip, or even planning a Friday night dinner out can become a mini planning exercise for you. You are only limited by your imagination and your commitment to learn the skill.

Regardless of the time available, you must always remember this principle: *see the terrain, see the enemy, see yourself.*

Troop Leading Procedures are a time management and organization tool to help you see the terrain, see the enemy, see yourself and craft a plan. Take a couple of minutes alone to gather your thoughts and figure out how you are going to do TLPs for that mission ("plan how you are going to plan") - then get after it.

After you view and evaluate the terrain and the enemy determine what your own actions should be in that situation. You must refresh your visualization continuously throughout the TLPs, basing your new mental "picture" of the AO on your refinements to the plan, additional information from sources, and/or developments from ongoing reconnaissance or security operations of parent or adjacent friendly units.

This process may seem kind of funky (and even frustrating) if you have prior mil experience and are used to receiving properly formatted orders. Orders produced through a formal process backed by leaders and staff with decades of experience. In the early phases of an event, you may not receive *any* orders; self-directed operations will be the norm. Even if your group is large enough to have a couple of echelons (eg a platoon with two or three squads) your highest echelon will most likely still be self-directing.

TLPs begin when the patrol leader gets indications of an upcoming operation and continues throughout the planning, preparation, and execution of the mission. He maximizes planning time by starting when the first bits of information are available. He uses no more than one-third of the available planning time to plan, prepare, and issue his order. This system of time allocation is known as the "one-third/two-thirds" rule of planning and preparation. This leaves a minimum of the remaining two-thirds of the time available for subordinates to conduct their own TLPs. Using the "one fifth/four fifths" approach is even better, the important thing is to allow your subordinates as much planning and prep time as possible. There is an art to knowing when you have enough information to release to subordinates (multiple WARNOs). More information is better, however there is a point when pushing ever changing info out becomes counterproductive and can create frustration among subordinate echelons. Experienced leaders will understand when it makes sense to push the next WARNO out to their subordinates.

Troop Leading Procedures (Overview)

This section briefly addresses the TLPs and is a high-level overview of the steps and some highlights of the process to assist with your mental model of how this process works.

The steps in the troop leading procedures are what the patrol leader will do to prepare the unit to accomplish a tactical mission. The 8 TLP steps are:

> 1. **Receive the mission.**
> 2. **Issue a warning order.**
> 3. **Make a tentative plan.**
> 4. **Initiate movement.**
> 5. **Conduct reconnaissance.**
> 6. **Complete the plan.**
> 7. **Issue the operations order.**
> 8. **Supervise and refine.**

The TLP starts when the leader is alerted to a mission or receives a change or new mission. Steps 3 through 8 are done in any order, or at the same time.

STEP 1. Receive the Mission

The leader may receive the mission in an OPORD or a FRAGO. The one third/two thirds rule (or 1/5 – 4/5) only applies to the planning and preparation section of time for an operation. Parallel planning occurs as the leader uses 1/3 of available planning and preparation time, and subordinates use the other 2/3. Parallel planning is when a subordinate or adjacent unit has enough information to plan simultaneously to save time. Emphasis is on conducting a hasty analysis with the primary focus on planning and preparation. You must do a detailed time analysis to determine the hours of daylight, planning time available, and help you and your team synchronize your efforts. An example time analysis is on the following page to give you an idea of the level of detail you need to get to as a patrol leader.

Reverse Planning Timeline

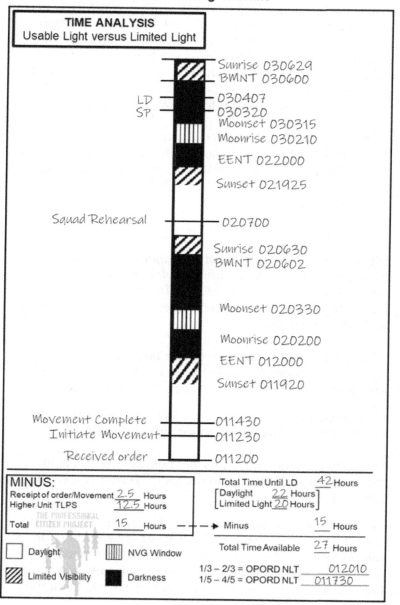

TIME ANALYSIS
Usable Light versus Limited Light

Sunrise 030629
BMNT 030600

LD — 030407
SP — 030320
Moonset 030315
Moonrise 030210

EENT 022000

Sunset 021925

Squad Rehearsal — 020700

Sunrise 020630
BMNT 020602

Moonset 020330

Moonrise 020200

EENT 012000

Sunset 011920

Movement Complete — 011430
Initiate Movement — 011230
Received order — 011200

MINUS:

Receipt of order/Movement 2.5 Hours
Higher Unit TLPS 12.5 Hours

THE PROFESSIONAL
CITIZEN PROJECT

Total 15 Hours — + — ►

☐ Daylight	⊞ NVG Window
▨ Limited Visibility	■ Darkness

Total Time Until LD 42 Hours
[Daylight 22 Hours]
[Limited Light 20 Hours]

Minus 15 Hours

Total Time Available 27 Hours

1/3 – 2/3 = OPORD NLT 012010
1/5 – 4/5 = OPORD NLT 011730

STEP 2. Issue a WARNO

The leader provides initial instructions in a WARNO that contains enough information for subordinates to begin preparation. The WARNO can be different formats, but generally it works well to mirror the five-paragraph OPORD format. The WARNO may include general location of the operation, timeline (both mission and planning), recon requirements, and information requirements.

STEP 3. Make a Tentative Plan

The patrol leader develops an estimate of the situation to use as the basis for the tentative plan. This is the leader's mission analysis done by using METT-TC to develop the tentative plan.

1. Conduct a detailed mission analysis:

Mission, intent, and concept of higher commanders' concepts and intents one and two levels up. This information is found in the OPORD you receive from your leadership, paragraph 1b for two levels up, and in paras 2 and 3 for one higher up.

Identify unit tasks. These are your tasks that are clearly stated in the order (specified tasks) or tasks that become apparent as the OPORD is analyzed (implied tasks).

Unit constraints. Identify any constraints placed on the unit that affects the ability to execute their missions.

Unit Limitations. The leader next determines all control measures or instructions in the OPORD that restrict his freedom of action.

Mission essential task(s). After reviewing all the factors shown in previous paragraphs, the leader identifies the mission essential task(s). This is especially important as failure to accomplish this task equals failure to accomplish the mission. The mission essential task should be in the maneuver paragraph.

Restated mission clearly and concisely states the mission (purpose to be achieved) and the mission essential task(s) required to achieve it. The restated mission statement becomes the focus for the remainder of the estimate process. It identifies WHO, WHAT (the task), WHEN (the critical time), WHERE (usually a grid coordinate), and WHY (the purpose the unit is to achieve).

Example of a restated mission:

(Who) 1st squad **(Task/What)** conducts Area Recon **(Where)** of OBJ RAPTOR vicinity NB 405262 **(When)** NLT 282230AUG24 **(Why)** IOT determine the risk to friendly convoy movement vic CHRISTIANSBURG.

(NLT- Not Later Than, IOT- In Order To, Vic- Vicinity)

2. Analyze the situation and develop a course of action (COA). A leader will brainstorm different ways to accomplish the mission and determine the requirements for the operation.

3. Complete generic task organization assigning all organic and attached elements. For example, you may allocate the USO or a HSW to a different fireteam or you may have assets attached from other units. You will also prepare the COA statement and sketch in this step. The COA statement clearly and concisely describes the COA sketch, it is a way for you to visualize the options inside the plan you are putting together. Together, the statement and sketch covers the *who* (generic task organization), *what* (tasks), *when*, *where*, and *why* (purpose) for all subordinate units and synchronizes their actions to accomplish the unit's mission while accounting for associated risk. The COA statement is easily translated into the details of paragraph 3 of your final OPORD.

4. With your restated mission to provide focus you will continue the estimate process using the remaining factors

145

of METT-TC. Inside of METT-TC analysis focus on what is known about the enemy and how he is arrayed on the terrain. METT-TC analysis is covered in depth in CM-1.

5. Analyze terrain using Observation and fields of fire, Avenues of approach, Key terrain, Obstacles, and Cover and concealment (OAKOC, the components are described in detail in CM-1. Keep in mind we look at terrain not just for terrain's sake, it is always a cause and effect relationship (how the terrain positively or negatively effects friendly and enemy forces) and how we can use the terrain to our advantage.

6. Analyze courses of action (Wargame). Wargaming is when the leader visualizes a set of actions, reactions, and counteractions. This analysis is conducted by wargaming your courses of action against the enemy's most probable courses of action. At company and lower echelons, we generally conduct a war game more intuitively than as a structured process as a large unit staff would do during MDMP. The object is to determine what can go wrong and what decision the leader will likely have to make as a result.

7. Compare courses of action. Compare the COAs and select the one that is most likely to accomplish the mission. Consider the advantages and disadvantages for each COA and how the critical events as the fight unfolds impact COAs.

8. Make a decision. Select the COA that you assess has the best chance of accomplishing the mission.

STEP 4. Initiate Movement; STEP 5. Conduct Reconnaissance; and STEP 6. Complete the Plan

The unit may need to begin movement while the patrol leader is still planning or forward reconnoitering. This step may occur anytime during the TLP. If time allows, the leader makes a personal reconnaissance.

When time does not allow, the leader conducts a map reconnaissance and sometimes the leader relies on others (such as senior team leader) to conduct the reconnaissance. The leader completes the plan based on the reconnaissance and any changes in the situation.

Complete the plan and fill out pre-formatted order shells. Other members of the squad must assist with this task in the interest of time (eg the HTL completes paragraph 4 and the RTO completes paragraph 5) for the patrol leader's review.

STEP 7. Issue the OPORD

Platoon and SLs normally issue oral operation orders to aid subordinates in understanding the concept for the mission. Doctrine states that if possible, leaders should issue the order within sight of the objective, on the defensive terrain, or on a terrain model or sketch. One quick thought on this, issuing an order in sight of your objective is tactically unsound. Decades of doing this none of us on our team have ever issued an offensive or recon order within sight of the objective; using a terrain model will be the most likely way you will issue your orders if on the offense.

Leaders may require subordinates to repeat all or part of the order, or demonstrate on the model or sketch, their understanding of the operation. They should also quiz their fighters to ensure that all understand the mission.

STEP 8. Supervise, Refine, and Rehearse

The leader supervises the unit's preparation for combat by conducting rehearsals and inspections. Rehearsals include the practice of having SLs brief their planned actions in execution sequence to the PL.

Rehearsals

Never underestimate the value of rehearsals. Rehearsals are one of the most valuable tools in preparing the patrol for the upcoming operation. ***Rehearsals are not for planning.*** The leader should conduct rehearsals on terrain that resembles the actual ground and in similar light conditions. The patrol leader uses well-planned, efficiently run rehearsals to accomplish the following purposes:

Reinforce training and increase proficiency in critical tasks.

Reveal weaknesses or problems in the plan.

Synchronize the actions of subordinate elements and improve each fighter's understanding of the concept of the operation.

The patrol may begin rehearsals of battle drills and other SOP items before the receipt of the operation order. Once the order has been issued, it can rehearse mission-specific tasks. Some important tasks to rehearse include:

Actions on the objective and actions at the patrol base or OP.

Marking obstacles (mine and wire) and using special weapons or field expedient demolitions (if available).

Actions on enemy contact.

The patrol leader can choose among several types of rehearsals, each designed to achieve a specific result and with a specific role in the planning and preparation timeline. Always keep in mind rehearsals are NOT planning. ***If you see a rehearsal devolve into a planning or second guessing session take the time***

to reassess the plan and reset. Adjustments and small refinements to the plan based on rehearsals are ok and should be made, just be self-aware and have a sense when these adjustments turn into planning or de-synchronize the original COA. This will only come with experience.

Location. Do not rehearse where the enemy can potentially observe you. Sounds like common sense, but I watched my brigade commander conduct a full brigade rehearsal out in the open during a training rotation in full view of opposing force (OPFOR) scouts. The second part of this is always sanitize any terrain model, the leave no trace philosophy is always in full effect for us. And remember unless you are in a cantonment area/secure facility you can't just pull everyone in for the rehearsal. Security must stay in place, so your subordinate leaders must do the work of catching up their team individually after the rehearsal. It is critical that everyone understands the mission and intent, especially in our small irregular units. We can't afford to leave anyone in the dark about a mission.

Rehearsal types

Current doctrine is all over the place on the types and techniques of rehearsals. There are lists of these categories from current doctrine that both complement and contradict one another. The info below may not match a familiar piece of doctrine, but it is a starting point to adjust your SOPs. The concept and the purpose are the important things to understand. As with all things in the CM manuals adjust to make it fit your requirements.

Confirmation brief. The confirmation brief is, in effect, a reverse briefing process routinely performed by subordinate leaders immediately after receiving any instructions, such as an OPORD or FRAGO. They confirm their understanding by repeating and explaining details of the operation for their leader. The patrol leader should conduct confirmation briefs after his subordinate leaders have received the OPORD, but before other phases of the patrol rehearsal begin.

Backbrief. Leaders perform this type of rehearsal throughout the planning and preparation timeline to help clarify their intent for their subordinates. The backbrief allows the patrol leader to identify problems in his own concept of the operation and his subordinates' understanding of the concept; he uses it to learn how subordinates intend to accomplish their missions.

Support rehearsal. Support rehearsals are normally conducted within the framework of a single warfighting function, such as fires or sustainment, or a limited number of warfighting functions. The goals are to ensure that support elements can achieve their missions within the higher commander's plan. For our purposes an example would be the HTL or platoon sergeant would conduct casualty evac rehearsals assisted by the medic(s).

Battle drill or SOP rehearsal. This type of rehearsal is used to ensure that all participants understand a technique or a specific set of procedures. The patrol leader or HTL initiates battle drill and/or SOP rehearsals as soon as possible after receipt of the mission; he then can continue to conduct them as needed throughout the planning. For example, the team leader(s) could rehearse procedures for marking obstacle lanes or establishing local security while the patrol leader is still working on his order. We recommended that you rehearse actions on contact drills frequently during planning and preparation.

Rehearsal Techniques

The patrol leader can choose among several techniques in conducting rehearsals, which should follow the crawl-walk-run training methodology to prepare the platoon for increasingly difficult conditions. Techniques for conducting rehearsals are limited only by the resourcefulness of the leader and the security conditions during mission prep. There are six basic techniques (full dress, reduced force, terrain model, sketch map, map, and radio).

The following discussion covers these techniques, which are listed in descending order in terms of the preparation time and resources required to conduct them. Considerations in selecting a rehearsal technique include Time (how much time will be needed for planning, preparation, and execution), Terrain (the applicable terrain considerations), multiechelon employment (how many echelons are involved and have you worked with them before), and Operations security (OPSEC) (will the rehearsal venue allow observation by the enemy or community agents to gain intelligence about upcoming operations).

Full force rehearsal. This rehearsal produces the most detailed understanding of the mission, but is the most difficult to conduct in terms of preparation and resources. It involves every team member and system participating in the operation. If possible, units should conduct the full force rehearsal under the same conditions (such as weather, time of day, terrain, and use of live ammunition) that they will encounter during the actual operation.

Reduced force or Key Leader rehearsal. This rehearsal normally involves only key leaders of the unit and is thus less extensive than the full dress rehearsal in terms of preparation time and resources. The commander decides the level of leader involvement. The selected leaders then rehearse the plan, if possible on the terrain to be used for the actual operation. The reduced force rehearsal is often conducted to prepare leaders for the full dress rehearsal.

Terrain model rehearsal. **This is the most used rehearsal technique**, employing an accurately constructed model for your patrol members to visualize the operation and fully understand the commander's intent for the mission. When possible, the patrol leader places the terrain model where it overlooks similar terrain of the AO or is within walking distance of such a vantage point (METT-TC dependent). The size of the model can vary, but it should be large enough to depict graphic control measures and important terrain features for reference and orientation. Participants walk or move icons around the table or model to practice the actions in relation to other members of the patrol. The terrain model must always be oriented and have a north seeking arrow, be a reasonable, easily understood representation of the terrain, be large enough to be of use, and accurately portray graphic controls measures.

Terrain model rehearsals are the most common for the small unit. They can be rudimentary or refined, just ensure they allow you to issue clear, concise orders to your team. Always sanitize the area afterwords and ensure you don't rehearse in an area exposed to enemy observation.

Sketch map or board rehearsal. Units can use the sketch map technique almost anywhere, day or night. Procedures are similar to those for the terrain model rehearsal. The sketch must be large enough to allow all participants to see as each subordinate "walks" through an interactive oral presentation of his actions. Patrol elements can use symbols or physical icons to represent their locations and maneuver on the sketch.

Map rehearsal. Procedures are similar to those for the sketch map rehearsal except that the commander or leader uses a map and operation overlay of the same scale as he used to plan and control the operation. This technique is useful in conjunction with a confirmation brief or backbrief involving subordinate leaders. The patrol leader uses the map and overlay to guide participants as they brief their role in the operation.

Radio rehearsal. This rehearsal simulates critical portions of the operation orally and interactively over established communications networks. The radio rehearsal may be especially useful when the situation does not allow the units to gather at one location. The radio rehearsal is probably not a viable method for the guerilla force due to direction finding and interception vulnerabilities. We have included it since it is doctrinally correct, and you may decide you can use components or the concept of it for your purposes. Deception or spoofing select FM comms during the rehearsal phase may be valuable to confuse the threat, but the DF issue cannot be dismissed if you decide to do this. Weigh the risks and decide if they outweigh the benefits of doing so.

Checks and Inspections

PCCs and PCIs allow leaders to check the patrol's readiness. The key goal is to ensure that fighters are fully prepared to execute the mission. The patrol leader makes sure the entire chain of command conducts PCCs and PCIs.

Precombat Checks. Equipment operators, vehicle crewmen, and individual fighters conduct PCCs before executing operations. These checks are designed to ensure that equipment is in working order, required supplies are on hand, and the team members are ready to execute the mission. PCCs are conducted in accordance with appropriate technical manuals and unit SOPs. Areas covered by PCCs include but are not limited to the following:

Preventive maintenance checks and services (PMCS) of essential equipment.

Inspections of load carrying equipment.

Medic / combat lifesaver bag inventories.

Resupply of rations, water, fuel, lubricants, all weapons, ammunition, pyrotechnics, first-aid kits, and equipment batteries (resupply or recharge status) for such items as flashlights, night vision devices.

Individual readiness. This includes ensuring that team members understand the mission and tactical situation and are in the correct uniform and tailored fighting load.

Prepare-to-fire checks for all weapons. This includes reporting or repairing deficiencies and making sure that weapons are functional and all sights are in good working order. Machine guns (if available) should be test-fired, if possible (METT-TC applies).

Communications checks, including radio, and tactical HF systems.

This includes verifying proper uploading of data (verifying AES 256 encryption keys for example), proper radio settings, charge levels of associated batteries, and integration of attached assets and digital systems.

Precombat Inspections. Leaders conduct PCIs to ensure that subordinate leaders and fighters have executed the necessary PCCs. Obviously, leaders cannot possibly check everything. They should focus on key pieces of equipment and details of the plan that are critical to mission accomplishment. The patrol leader and senior TL / HTL should coordinate their inspections to make optimum use of available time and to avoid redundant inspections. PCIs must be completed in time to fix deficiencies before mission execution begins. Squad or Team leaders should conduct initial inspections shortly after receipt of the WARNO. The senior Team Leader spot checks throughout the unit's preparation for combat. The patrol leader and HTL make a final inspection. Precombat checks and inspection include:

- Weapons and ammunition.

- Uniforms and equipment.

- Mission-essential equipment.

- Individual understanding of the mission, intent, and individual responsibilities.

- Communications.

- Rations and water.

- Camouflage.

- Deficiencies noted during earlier inspections.

Assumption of Command

Any patrol or squad member might have to take command of his element in an emergency, so every team member must be prepared to do so. Paragraph 5 of the WARNO and OPORD must designate this contingency and every member must be prepared to take charge. During an assumption of command, situation permitting, the individual assuming command accomplishes the tasks (not necessarily in this order), based on METT-TC shown in the following table:

Tasks for assumption of command	
INFORMS	The unit's subordinate leaders of the command and notifies higher
CHECKS	Security
CHECKS	Crew-served weapons
PINPOINTS	Location (know where you are)
COORDINATES AND CHECKS	Equipment
CHECKS	Personnel status
ISSUES	Fragmentary order (FRAGO), if required
REORGANIZES	As needed, maintaining unit integrity when possible
MAINTAINS	Noise and light discipline
CONTINUES	Patrol base activities, especially security, if assuming command in a patrol base
RECON	At the very least conduct a map reconnaissance
FINALIZES	Plan

Order Formats

The art and science of writing and briefing orders is a skill that only develops with lots of practice. Just as we recommended for planning, take what seems like odd opportunities to practice writing orders. Those road trips, range days, family vacations etc. Have your teammates review them and give you feedback. Conduct tabletop and map exercises with your team using scenarios so all of you can practice generating and issuing orders. Replicate field conditions when doing these exercises, use only what you carry in the field. Learning the skill will come, focus first on learning and becoming an expert at TLPs overall. The order process is part of this of course, but understanding and using the time and information management benefits of TLPs will pay the most dividends for you early on.

The generic order formats on the following pages can be used to build blank shells for field use. A "shell" is the term for an unfilled order outline with space to write in the information, they can be invaluable time savers for leaders. These are not checklists, but they will assist you with following the established formats that are consistently used and familiar in the profession.

Who else needs to know? Don't forget to keep your security teams up to speed with info, always know who got the order brief and who hasn't yet. Rotate them out and brief the order twice if you have to.

Sample WARNO Format ("A" Way)

WARNO Format
Roll call, pencil, pen, paper, map, protractor, leader's monitor, hold all questions until the end. References: refer to higher HQ OPORD and identify map sheet for operation. Time zone used throughout the order: (optional) Task organization: optional, see para 1c.
1. **SITUATION.** Find this in higher HQ OPORD para 1a (1-3). Include the following information: a. **Area of interest:** outline the area of interest on the map. 　Orient relative to each point on the compass (north, south, east, and west). 　Box in the entire area of operation (AO) with grid lines. b. **Area of operations:** outline the area of operation on the map. Point out the objective and current location of your unit. 　Trace your zone using boundaries. 　Familiarize by identifying natural (terrain) and man-made features in the zone your unit is operating. c. **Enemy forces:** include significant changes in enemy composition, dispositions, and courses of action. Information not available for inclusion in the initial WARNORD can be included in subsequent warning orders (WHO, WHAT, WHERE). d. **Friendly forces:** optional, address only if essential to the WARNORD. 　Give higher commander's mission (WHO, WHAT, WHEN, WHERE, WHY). 　State higher commander's intention. (Higher HQ [go to map board] OPORD para 1b[2]), give task and purpose. 　Point out friendly locations on the map board. e. **Attachments and detachments:** give initial task organization, only address major unit changes, and then go to the map board.
2. **MISSION.** State mission twice (who, what, when, where, why).

WARNO Format (cont'd)

3. **EXECUTION.** Include the following information:

a. **Concept of operations:** provide as much information as available. The concept should describe the employment of maneuver elements. Give general direction, estimated distance, estimated time of travel, mode of travel, and major tasks to be conducted. Cover all movements, and specify points where the ground tactical plan starts and stops.

b. **Tasks to subordinate units:** provide specific tasks to subordinate units to aid in planning, preparing, and executing the mission. Planning guidance consists of tasks assigned to elements in the form of teams, special teams, and key individuals.

c. **Coordinating instructions:** include any information available at that time, if known. At least cover the following items:

Uniform and equipment common to all.

Consider the factors of METT-TC and tailor the load for each fighter.

Timeline. (State when, what, where, who and all specified times).

Reverse plan. Use one-third to two-thirds rule.

Give specific priorities in order of completion.

Give information about coordination meetings.

Rehearsals and inspections by priority.

Earliest movement time.

4. **SUSTAINMENT.** Include any known logistics preparation for the operation.

a. **Logistics:** include the following information:

Maintenance: include weapons and equipment direct exchange (DX) time and location.

Transportation: state method and mode of transportation for infiltration and exfiltration. Identify any coordination needed for external assets. Task subordinate leader (if needed) to generate load plan, number of lifts or serials, and bump plan.

Supply: only include classes of supply that require coordination or special instructions (such as rations, fuel, ammunition, or other items).

b. **Health support:** identify any medical equipment, support, or preventative medicine that needs to be coordinated.

WARNO Format (cont'd)

5. COMMAND AND SIGNAL.

a. **Command:** state the succession of command, if not covered in the unit's SOP.

b. **Control:** include the following information:

Command posts: describe the employment of CPs, including the location of each CP and its time of opening and closing, as appropriate. Typically, at platoon level, the only reference to command posts is the company CP.

Reports: list reports not covered in the SOP.

Signal: describe the concept of signal support, including current signal operating instructions (SOI) edition or refer to the higher OPORD. Give subordinates guidance on tasks to complete for preparation of the OPORD and the mission.

Give time, place, and uniform for the OPORD. Give a time hack and ask for questions.

Sample OPORD Format ("A" Way)

TASK ORGANIZATION (how the unit is organized for the mission).

PARAGRAPH 1. SITUATION.
a. Weather and light data.
(1) Light conditions: BMNT: , Sunrise: , Sunset: ; EENT: , Moonrise: , Moonset: ; Percent Illumination: .
(2) Weather forecast for the operation.
(3) Effects of weather and light conditions on the operation.
(a) Trafficability.
(b) Visibility.
(c) Effect on lasers/thermals
b. Terrain.
(1) Obstacles, hills, valleys, road types and conditions,
streams, rivers, bridges, built-up areas.
(2) Avenues of approach.
(a) Size unit that can be supported. (b) Start and end point.
(c) Objective.
(3) Key terrain (discuss how friendly and/or enemy forces may attempt to use it to their advantage).
(4) Observation and fields of fire. (5) Cover and concealment.
(6) Engagement areas.
(7) Overall effect of terrain on the operation.

c. Enemy forces.
(1) Identification.
(2) Activity. (3) Location. (4) Disposition. (5) Strength.
(6) Composition, to include type and capabilities of equipment. (7) Other enemy information critical to the upcoming operation, to include the following:
(a) Artillery, mortar, and obstacle capabilities.
(b) Air defense.
(c) Aviation, including helicopters. (d) Electronic warfare.
(8) Enemy courses of action (discussion should focus on identifying enemy's most probable courses of action).
d. Friendly forces (include the following items as applicable).
(1) Mission of higher headquarters (your parent unit), including commander's intent and scheme of maneuver. (This may include a review of the next higher unit scheme of maneuver or commander's intent.)
(2) ID/mission of adjacent units (left, right, front, rear).
(3) ID/mission of reserves in higher headquarters.
(4) ID/mission of supporting units (supply, medical etc).
(5) Which higher headquarters element has priority of support (consolidated UAS, supply, medical, etc).
(6) Additional assets allocated to higher headquarters, including number and type available.
e. Attachments and detachments (who was added from the outside and who you may be giving up to another unit/team)

PARAGRAPH 2. Mission. This is the WHO, WHAT, WHEN, WHERE, and WHY of the operation. State essential task(s) to be accomplished by the entire unit, to include on-order missions. Clearly define the platoon's objective.

PARAGRAPH 3. Execution.
a. Intent. Using the commander's intent as a guideline, the leader defines the purpose, key tasks, and end state of the operation. The purpose defines the WHY of the operation. The key tasks (the "method") describes how the leader visualizes achieving success with respect to the mission as a whole; it also outlines, in general terms, how he plans to use any combat multipliers. The end state specifies the final disposition of forces and explains how the end state will facilitate future operations.
b. Concept of the operation. The concept statement further explains and expands on the platoon leader's (and/or commander's) intent, particularly his vision of HOW he will conduct the operation and WHO he will assign to execute it. The leader uses the concept statement when he feels more detail is necessary to ensure subordinates will take the appropriate actions in the absence of additional communications or further orders.
The sequence of subparagraphs is as follows:
(1) Scheme of maneuver. This is how the unit will maneuver to accomplish its mission. It conforms with the commander's intent. In offensive operations, it specifies the formation, movement technique, routes or avenues of advance, and plans for direct fire and overwatch. In defensive operations, it specifies the engagement plan, battle positions, orientation of weapons, and the plan for movement to subsequent positions.

(2) Fires.

(a) Purpose for artillery and mortar fires (how fires will be used to support the maneuver). You will see this in formats, while it most likely will not apply you should still be familiar with it).

(b) Priority of fires within the unit.

(c) Allocation of final protective fires.

(d) Preparation starting time and duration of fires.

(e) Triggers (trigger line/point or event).

(f) Enemy fires landing in the area of operations.

(g) Allocation/use of other fires (smoke/illumination/CAS).

(h) Restrictions.

(3) Engineer support (obstacles, mines, fortifications).

(a) Priority of engineer effort (mobility, countermobility, survivability).

(b) Priority of engineer support.

(c) Obstacle overlay and obstacle list.

(d) Logistical constraints.

(e) On-order missions.

c. Specific instructions. List specific missions, in "battle sequence," for each element, including attached elements. Include movement techniques, flank coordination requirements, other details, and "be prepared to" missions.

d. Coordinating instructions.

(1) Time schedule for critical events.

(a) Rehearsals and confirmation briefings (back-briefs).

(b) PCI.

(c) First movement.

(d) Arrival of any attachments/detachments.

(2) Movement instructions.

(3) Passage of lines.

(a) Contact points and passage points.

(b) Lanes, to include identification/markings.

(4) Actions at danger areas.
(5) Actions on expected contact.
(6) Rally points.
(7) ROE (Rules of Engagement) and weapons status.
(8) PIR.
(9) Air defense warning and weapon control status.
(10) Be-prepared tasks or other information not provided in concept of the operation or specific instructions.

PARAGRAPH 4. Service Support.
a. Location and movement plan of any supply assets
b. Material and services.
(1) Supply.
(a) Priorities of supply (who gets resupplied first).
(b) Resupply points and prestock (cache) sites.
(c) Ration cycle (chow plan while the unit is out)
(d) Location of parent unit logistics team (if applicable).
(2) Transportation.
(a) Supply routes.
(b) LRPs (any preplanned reupply points).
(c) Priorities established on MSRs.
(3) Services. Handling of KIAs.
(4) Maintenance.
(a) Maintenance support available for equipment.
c. Medical evacuation and treatment.
(1) Location of medics, aid station (if present), and ambulance exchange points.
(2) Procedures for treatment and evacuation of WIAs.
(3) Aeromedical evacuation information (probably will not be available; plan during training for lifeflights).
(4) Handling of contaminated WIAs (chemical or suspected bio).

d. Personnel.
(1) Handling and disposition instructions for EPWs.
(2) EPW guard instructions.
(3) Location of EPW collection point.
(4) Instructions for interaction with local civil populace (based on applicable ROE).
(5) Number of expected replacements (expect zero).
(6) Cross-leveling procedures.
e. Miscellaneous.

PARAGRAPH 5. Command and Signal.
a. Command.
(1) Location of the leaders during the operation to include higher HQ), as well as location of command posts.
(2) Succession of command.
b. Signal.
(1) SOI index and edition in effect (code series, OTPs).
(a) Key frequencies (AES key if used)
(b) Key call signs.
(c) Current item number identifier.
(2) Crypto fill and changeover data (for any electronic encryption).
(3) Listening silence instructions.
(4) Challenge and password to include running password
(5) Special signals, to include use of pyrotechnics.
(6) Code words.
(7) Digital traffic instructions (digital systems only}.
(8) Actions to counteract jamming or "hot mike" situations.
TIME CHECK (always use GPS or atomic clock time).

Chapter 5
Movement

Route Selection and Planning

These principles apply to moving as an individual, small teams, or movement in larger tactical formations. OAKOC always applies, and as you develop your skills you will be able to visualize the route over the terrain. (Detailed route planning is done during TLPs). Portions of these concepts are also in CM-1, the importance of understanding and applying these principles warrants expanding on in this manual.

Move During Limited Visibility. As discussed in the night scouting section, movement during darkness or other limited visibility conditions can provide concealment from the enemy. Combining a route's characteristics with the advantages of poor weather or limited visibility advantages during night can work in our favor.

Legs. By breaking the overall route into several smaller segments, you are able to manage the longer route during your movement. Legs typically have only one distance and direction. A change in direction will end the leg and begin a new one. These can be azimuths (dead reckoning) or by terrain association. At night these will be shorter to make them manageable and keep navigation confidence high.

Bypassing an Obstacle or Danger Area. To bypass enemy positions or obstacles and still stay oriented, detour around the obstacle by moving at right angles for specified distances or use terrain association to contour around the open danger area. METT-TC applies of course. Your team must have a well-rehearsed battle drill for crossing or bypassing danger areas. These should not be significant as to become "an event", the unit should flow through the drill smoothly and continue mission.

Use Terrain for Protection. Dismounted movement techniques can help units use the terrain over which they move to their advantage. Avoid "skylining" or moving near the top of a ridge or hill while silhouetting yourself. Choose routes that do not stand out and avoid *natural lines of drift* through terrain (avoid the easiest path). Plan routes to take advantage of disruptions in line of sight from the templated enemy's perspective. Using an approach that uses the side or lower contours of a hill or ridge vs exposing the patrol by going directly over must be planned for during TLPs. This is where the detailed work during your OAKOC terrain analysis comes in, for a dismounted force we have to look at this with an eye for detail.

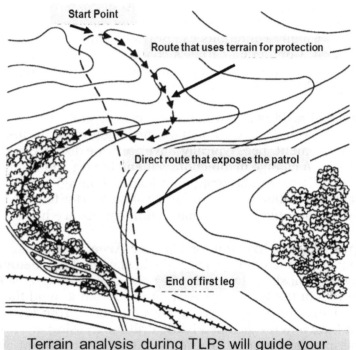

Terrain analysis during TLPs will guide your route selection. Set your legs up to take advantage of terrain that disrupts line of sight from suspected enemy locations.

168

Avoid Possible Kill Zones. Avoid large open areas surrounded by cover and concealment or those dominated by a piece of terrain that the enemy would likely use. If you would select it as an ambush site it is best to not traverse that piece of ground.

Backstop/ Handrail. A backstop is an easily identifiable terrain or man made feature that swill indicate you have gone too far beyond your destination or checkpoint. A handrail is similar to the backstop but they run parallel or partially parallel to your desired route and will indicate departure from your route laterally. These can also be used (if the tactical situation dictates) to guide navigation by walking to the side but within visual of the feature.

Attack Point. An easily recognizable feature that is a few hundred meters from your end point / objective that you can easily find. You will use the attack point to "reset" your nav route, they can assist with finding more difficult objectives that may not be near an identifiable feature. Once you reach your attack point double check your location and then execute the final short leg you had already planned. This shorter (and more manageable) leg will bring you to your final objective such as the ORP or patrol base.

Tactical Movement

Tactical movement involves movement of a unit assigned a mission under combat conditions when not in direct ground contact with the enemy. Tactical movement is based on the anticipation of early ground contact with the enemy, either enroute or shortly after arrival at the destination. Movement ends when ground contact is made or the unit reaches its destination. *Movement is not maneuver.* Maneuver is conducted while in contact, supported by fire, to gain a position of advantage over the enemy.

169

Dismounted Formations

The basics of formations and techniques of movement are covered in depth in CM-1. Standard formations are a good starting point for learning and developing applicable SOPs for your team. The non-standard force will not be a direct lift from these as you and *your unit may move and operate in a different manner.* However, there are many fundamentals and principles from these that can be applied to your training. The advantages attributed to one of these formations may be disadvantages to another. Knowing the advantages and applications of these is required to adjust for terrain and enemy situation (METT-TC applies as always). Each does so with different degrees of emphasis resulting in unique advantages and disadvantages. Do not be rigid in the application of these; variations and modifications should be experimented with and proven out during your training. Keep your tactics grounded in fundamental concepts, train, and rehearse so everyone understands what they are doing and more importantly why they are doing it. Apply some common tactical sense and it does not matter if a formation or tactic doesn't exactly match the accepted doctrine. Ideas that are not tactically sound do not fall into this category.

The recurring theme is always do what works for you and your group; don't train from a place of fear that a particular method will not be legitimate because it does not look exactly like doctrine.

Formations with more than one lead element are better for achieving fire superiority to the front but are more difficult to control. Conversely, formations with only one lead element are easier to control but are not as useful for achieving fire superiority to the front.

170

Leaders must maintain flexibility in their formations to enable them to react when unexpected enemy actions occur.

The term formation refers to your relative position within the unit and how the patrol is arrayed on the battlefield as they move across various terrain. Regardless of which formation the team employs, each person must know his location in the formation relative to the other fire team members and team leader and patrol leader. Each individual covers a set area of responsibility for observation and direct fire as the team is moving. To provide the unit with all-around protection, these areas interlock. Team leaders are constantly aware of their teams' sectors of fire and correct them as required, the HTL will ensure the patrol has interlocking fields of observation and fire when occupying patrol bases.

The patrol leader adjusts the formation as necessary while the formation is moving. The distance between individuals is determined by the mission, the nature of the threat, the closeness of the terrain, and visibility. As a general rule, the formation should be dispersed up to the limit of control. This allows for a wide area to be covered, makes the patrol's movement difficult to detect, and makes it less vulnerable to enemy attack.

Fire teams, squads, and platoons use several formations. Formations give the leader control, based on a METT-TC analysis. Leaders position themselves where they can best command and direct the formations, which are shown in the figure below. Typical formations are the line, vee, echelon, diamond, wedge, and file.

Formations allow the fire team leaders and patrol leader to lead by example. (Follow me and do as I do) All members in the team must be able to see their leader, team leaders must be able to see the patrol leader (this ebbs and flows with terrain and movement technique). Every individual has a standard position in a formation that allows seamless operations with other friendly forces. Leaders control their units using arm-and hand signals, verbal commands during contact, and intra-squad/team communications (on a very limited basis due to electronic signature). When squads operate in wedges or in echelon, the fire teams use those formations and simply arrange themselves in a column or with one team behind the other. Squads / patrols may also use the vee, where one team forms the lines of the vee with the squad leader at the front (at the point of the vee) for mission command.

FORMATIONS

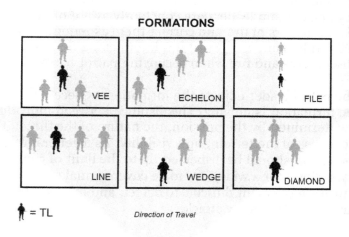

⫯ = TL   *Direction of Travel*

The interval between individuals in the wedge formation is approximately 10 meters but the wedge expands and contracts depending on the terrain and the movement technique at any given time. This fundamental practice applies to all the formations a patrol uses. Patrols modify the formation when rough terrain, poor visibility, or other factors make control difficult. The normal interval is reduced so all team members still can see their team leader and all team leaders still can see their squad or patrol leader. For example, the sides of the wedge can contract to the point where the wedge resembles a single file as you move through dense vegetation. Team members expand or resume their original positions when moving in less rugged terrain where control is easier.

In the wedge formation the fire team leader is in the lead position with his team members echeloned to the right and left behind him. The positions for all but the leader may vary. You may have HSW, designated marksman, machine gunners (things may develop to make belt feds a possibility), unmanned aerial and ground controllers (the USO), and snipers inside our non-standard / guerilla formations. Placing these assets inside of formations is the responsibility of the leader, he will adjust assets location based on METT-TC. All formations still permit the fire team leader to lead by example; his standing order to his team is always "Follow me and do as I do." When he moves to the left, his team should move to the left. When he fires, his team fires. When using the lead-by-example technique, it is essential for all individuals to maintain visual contact with their leader and cue off his actions.

Everyone in a formation has their sector of responsibility to scan. Sometimes those individual sectors don't align with weapon orientation, but that is ok (right hander with right side sector).

173

Rolling T

Scouts can modify the wedge formation when terrain dictates, and a common modified formation is the rolling T formation. The rolling T formation still provides good firepower to the front and sides, but places some scouts behind each other like the file. The rolling T formation provides good control for the formation especially when operating in sparse vegetation / open areas. This works well for the HQ Team inside a Squad column when the two other fire teams are in wedges.

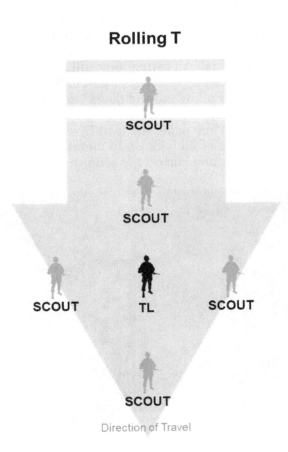

Rolling T

SCOUT

SCOUT

SCOUT   TL   SCOUT

SCOUT

Direction of Travel

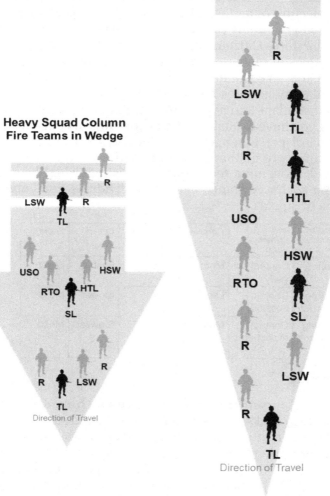

Heavy Squad Column Fire Teams in Wedge

R

LSW   R
TL

USO   HSW
   RTO HTL
      SL

      R
R   LSW
   TL
Direction of Travel

Heavy Squad Modified Wedge

R

LSW   TL

R   HTL

USO   HSW

RTO   SL

R   LSW

R
   TL
Direction of Travel

Movement Techniques

There are three movement techniques: ***traveling; traveling overwatch; and bounding overwatch.*** The selection of a movement technique is based on the likelihood of enemy contact and the need for speed. As an irregular force Citizens may adapt formations and techniques of movement for use down to two- and three-man teams. We will discuss this section in terms of squads since it demonstrates the different options well, however you must adapt and adjust this baseline for the team and assets you have available. The factors to consider include control, dispersion, speed, and security. Movement techniques are neither fixed nor are they formations. Instead, movement techniques are distinguished by a set of criteria such as distance between individuals and between teams or squads.

MOVEMENT TECHNIQUES	WHEN NORMALLY USED	Control	Dispersion	Speed	Security
Traveling	Contact not likely	More	Less	Fastest	Least
Traveling Overwatch	Contact possible	Less	More	Slower	More
Bounding Overwatch	Contact expected	Most	Most	Slowest	Most

Traveling

Traveling is ***used when contact with the enemy is not likely*** and speed is required for the mission. As illustrated in the diagram on the next page the SL is positioned where he can direct both teams with approximately 20 meters (METT-TC dependent) between SL and B TM Leader. When using the traveling technique, all unit elements move continuously. In continuous movement, all individuals travel at a moderate rate of speed, with all personnel alert. During traveling, formations are essentially not altered except for effects of terrain.

176

9 Man Squad Traveling

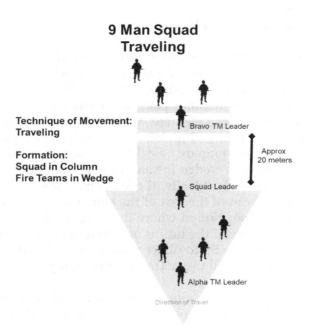

Technique of Movement:
Traveling

Formation:
Squad in Column
Fire Teams in Wedge

Bravo TM Leader

Approx
20 meters

Squad Leader

Alpha TM Leader

Direction of Travel

Heavy Squad Traveling

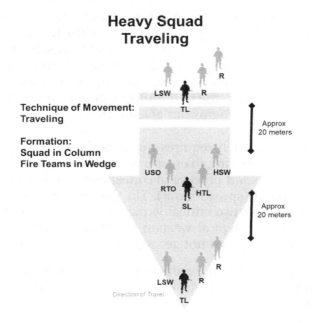

Technique of Movement:
Traveling

Formation:
Squad in Column
Fire Teams in Wedge

R
LSW   R
TL

Approx
20 meters

USO   HSW
RTO   HTL
SL

Approx
20 meters

R
LSW   R
TL

Direction of Travel

177

Traveling Overwatch

Traveling overwatch is ***used when contact is possible.***
This is an extended form of traveling in which the lead
element moves continuously but trailing elements move at
varying speeds, sometimes pausing to overwatch
movement of the lead element. Crew served or special
weapons move near and under the control of the squad
leader so they can employ quickly. Rifle squads normally
move in column or wedge formation with 20 meters
between individuals. Ideally, the lead team moves at least
50 meters in front of the rest of the element. The trail team
and the SL are positioned where they will not become
decisively engaged if the unit is attacked or ambushed. This
distance allows the SL to direct remaining elements to the
enemy's flank should the A Tm become engaged.

The trail element maintains dispersion based on its ability
to provide immediate suppressive fires to support the lead
element. The intent is to maintain depth, flexibility, and
sustain movement in case the lead element is engaged. The
trailing elements cue their movement to the terrain,
overwatching from a position where they can support the
lead element if needed. The idea is to put enough distance
between the lead and trail units so if the lead element
comes into contact, the trail unit(s) will have the ability to
maneuver on the enemy out of contact.

Traveling overwatch requires the leader to control his
subordinate's spacing to ensure mutual support. This
involves a constant process of concentrating (close it up)
and dispersion (spread it out). The desire is mutual
support, with its two critical variables being weapon ranges
and terrain. Our typical weapon range limitations dictate
(generally) we should not get separated by more than

2-300 meters (terrain dependent). In compartmentalized
terrain this distance is closer, but in open terrain this
distance is greater.

9 Man Squad
Traveling Overwatch

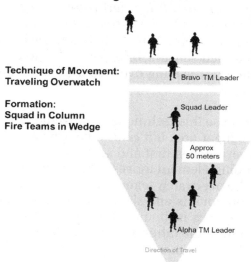

Technique of Movement:
Traveling Overwatch

Formation:
Squad in Column
Fire Teams in Wedge

Bravo TM Leader

Squad Leader

Approx
50 meters

Alpha TM Leader

Direction of Travel

Heavy Squad
Traveling Overwatch

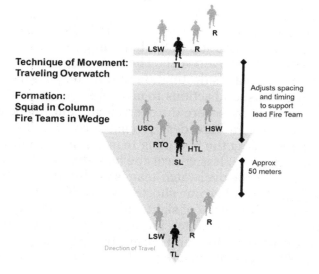

Technique of Movement:
Traveling Overwatch

Formation:
Squad in Column
Fire Teams in Wedge

R
LSW   R
TL

Adjusts spacing
and timing
to support
lead Fire Team

USO   HSW
RTO   HTL
SL

Approx
50 meters

R
LSW   R
TL

Direction of Travel

179

Bounding Overwatch

Bounding overwatch is used when contact is expected, the patrol leader assesses the enemy is near based upon movement, noise, reflection, trash, fresh tracks, unmanned sensors, or experience and transitions from traveling or traveling overwatch to bounding overwatch.

You may also use this technique of movement to cross a large open danger area if it cannot be bypassed. The lead fire team overwatches first and scans for enemy positions as the bounding element moves. The squad leader usually stays with the overwatch team to best direct the TLs. The trail fire team bounds and signals the squad leader when his team completes its bound and is prepared to overwatch the movement of the other team ("leap frog"). The bounding element can use traveling overwatch, bounding overwatch, or individual movement techniques (low and high crawl, and three- to five-second rushes by the fire team or buddy teams). The length of a bound depends on the terrain, visibility, and control.

Fire team leaders must know which team the squad leader is moving with. The overwatching team leader must know the route and destination of the bounding team as well so he can position his overwatch. The bounding team leader must know his team's destination and route, possible enemy locations, and actions to take when he arrives there. He also must know where the overwatch team will be and how he will receive his orders. Available cover and concealment along the bounding team's route dictates how its members move. It is critical the bounding team does not maneuver past the overwatch team's ability to support them. Bounds will become shorter as terrain and vegetation restrict lines of sight and create dead space that would render the overwatch ineffective. The overwatch team must be set before and during the bounding element's movement, ensure you have visual signals in your SOPs to support this requirement. This technique of movement can be employed by all size elements (up to a point). Small teams can use bounding overwatch to cover movement under the same conditions, but the tolerance for separation will be greatly reduced for smaller elements. This is due to the risk of separation and the consequences of single or two man elements being engaged in relative isolation during a bound.

The Bounding Overwatch concept works from buddy teams up through company level. One element is always stationary and can provide direct fire support for the moving element.

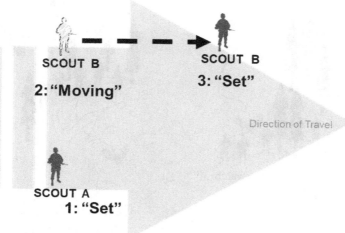

SCOUT B

2: "Moving"

SCOUT B

3: "Set"

Direction of Travel

SCOUT A

1: "Set"

Types of bounds

Successive bounds. One element moves to a position, and then the overwatching element moves to a position generally online with the first element. The leader can alternate the initial bounding element based on METT-TC factors but both end up generally aligned across the front line trace after bounds.

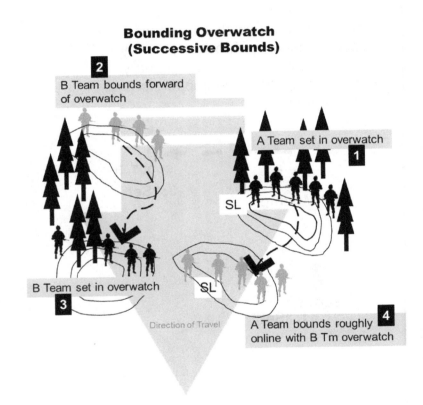

Bounding Overwatch
(Successive Bounds)

2 B Team bounds forward of overwatch

A Team set in overwatch **1**

SL

B Team set in overwatch **3**

SL

Direction of Travel

A Team bounds roughly online with B Tm overwatch **4**

Alternating bounds. A Team moves to and sets overwatch position, and then B Team bounds to a position forward (in relation to direction of movement) of A Team. This "leapfrog" continues during the movement.

Bounding Overwatch
(Alternating Bounds)

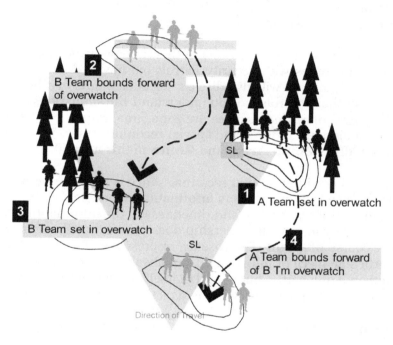

Before a bound, the leader gives the following instructions to subordinates:

- Direction of the enemy, if known.
- Position of overwatch elements.
- Next overwatch position.
- Route of the bounding element.
- What to do after the bounding element reaches the next position.
- How the elements receive follow-on orders.

Chapter 6
Recon Patrols

In simple terms patrols are missions to gather information or to conduct combat operations. A patrol is a detachment of company or smaller size sent out to gather information (recon) or carry out a destructive, harassing, or security mission (ambush, raid etc).

We will focus on recon patrols in this chapter (which share many attributes with Security Patrols but have a different purpose), and we will also discuss select elements of other types of these patrols, so you understand the similarities. The forms of reconnaissance are zone, area, route, reconnaissance in force and special reconnaissance. We will address **Zone, Area,** and **Route** in this manual.

Always keep in mind that reconnaissance is *not* decisive in and of itself; it only gathers information to enable decisive actions. It is the quality and timeliness of the information and what you or your leadership does with it that changes the course of a fight. The absence or presence of a particular piece of information can absolutely change the outcome of a battle, but in and of itself conducting a recon is only a small part of achieving a tactical victory.

Terms in this Section

Graphic Control Measure(s). GCMs or "Graphics" are scale drawings used on a map that facilitate shared understanding or a common language (eg Phase Lines, LD, NAIs, Objectives, OPs etc). Having a set of graphics allows a leader to synchronize his unit while providing another means to create common understanding for the team. Once we understand what a graphic means we immediately understand what the leader needs us to do (or not do). For example, an NAI on a map means that you are looking at that area for a specific piece of information that will confirm or deny an enemy COA. This all this together with what we have discussed in here; we look for things intentionally for a reason that will help a leader make a decision. A graphic will further assist us doing so; a simple box with three letters or a line with a name can replace a paragraph of redundant explanation in an OPORD.

Rally Point. A rally point is a place designated by the leader where the platoon moves to reassemble and reorganize if it becomes dispersed. The leader physically reconnoiters routes to select rally points whenever possible. He selects tentative points if he only can conduct a map reconnaissance. Routes are confirmed by the leader through actual inspection as the patrol moves through them. Rally points must be easy to recognize on the ground, have cover and concealment, be away from natural lines of drift, and be defendable for short periods.

Objective Rally Point (ORP). The ORP is a point out of sight, sound, and small-arms range of the objective area. It normally is located in the direction the patrol plans to move after completing its actions on the objective. The objective rally point typically lies 200 to 400 m from the objective, or at a minimum, one major terrain feature away. The ORP is tentative until the objective is pinpointed. Actions at or from the ORP include:

Issuing a final fragmentary order (FRAGO).

Disseminating information from reconnaissance.

Making final preparations before continuing operations.

Accounting for Scouts and equipment after actions at the objective are complete.

En route rally point. The leader designates en route rally points based on the terrain, vegetation, and visibility. These are pointed out via hand and arm signal as the patrol passes the rally point. This gives you a "meet back here if things go bad"; a rally point is a place designated by the leader where the unit moves to reassemble and reorganize if it becomes dispersed. Scouts know which rally point to move to at each phase of the patrol mission should they become separated from the unit. Default is always to the last one, your team SOP must account for contingencies and use of en route rally points. They also know what actions are required there and how long they are to wait at each rally point before moving to another.

Probable Line of Contact (PLOC). The PLOC is the geographic point at which the templated enemy's weapon systems can engage friendly forces. It is drawn as an irregular phase line to assist the patrol leader with changing formations or the technique of movement. This can be especially useful when siting OPs and developing an observation plan for an Area Reconnaissance objective.

Patrolling or conducting a patrol is the semi-independent operation conducted to accomplish the patrol's mission. A patrol requires a specific task and purpose. It must be prepared to secure itself, navigate accurately, identify and cross danger areas, and reconnoiter the patrol objective. If it is a combat patrol, it must be prepared to breach obstacles, assault the objective, and support those assaults by fire. Any type of patrol must be able to conduct detailed searches as well as deal with casualties and prisoners or detainees.

Reconnaissance patrols

Recon patrols are tasked to gather detailed information (the Priority Information Requirements (PIR) discussed before) on the enemy, terrain, or specific NAIs or enemy avenues of approach. We must improvise and adapt these techniques to units smaller than platoon size due to the personnel and unit size challenges we discussed at the start of this manual. There is no difference in the basics of reconnaissance, using smaller units will however require some creative thought to mitigate the lack of resources (both personnel and combat multipliers). Smaller areas, missions of shorter duration, judicious cueing of assets, and consolidation of security are all considerations for our smaller organizations.

Combat patrols

A combat patrol provides security and harasses, destroys, or captures enemy troops, equipment, or installations. When a leader assigns a combat patrol to a unit, he intends the patrol to make contact with the enemy and engage in close combat. A combat patrol collects and reports information gathered during the mission, whether related to the combat task or not. The three types of combat patrols are **raid, ambush, and security patrol**. A larger unit such as a platoon may conduct a combat patrol as part of the counter reconnaissance effort, though this type of patrol is not doctrinally common for platoon and smaller because of the personnel and resources required. If combat patrols are routinely required larger elements with conventional enablers should be tasked to conduct them.

A combat patrol always tries to remain undetected while moving, but when it discloses its location to the enemy it is with a sudden and violent attack. For this reason, the patrol normally carries a significant amount of weapons and ammunition.

Security Patrol. A security patrol is a type of combat patrol that is sent out from a unit location when the unit is stationary or during a halt to search the local area, detect enemy forces near the main body, and to engage and destroy the enemy within the capability of the patrol. Doctrinally the security patrol is a patrol is one that goes out "looking for a fight." For our purposes the patrols we will most likely conduct will fall somewhere between reconnaissance and security patrols especially when conducting "property patrols" that we discuss in the community so often.

Although this form of combat patrol seeks to make direct enemy contact and to destroy enemy forces within its capability, it must avoid decisive engagement. They do not operate beyond the range of communications from the main body.

They may be conducted either outside of friendly positions to provide early warning of enemy activity, or internally to prevent sabotage or attacks inside the perimeter of a facility. The requirement to conduct security patrols increases in static areas such as neighborhoods, protected sanctuaries, and other facilities that are commonly occupied by the community members.

Tracking patrols. A tracking patrol is a special type of patrol conducted to follow the trail of a specific enemy unit, though this is a relatively rare assignment. In this role, scouts look for signs left by the enemy. As they track the enemy unit, they gather information about the route and surrounding terrain. Having team members who are tracking experts and have formal training could be an invaluable asset to your team.

Patrolling Principles

All patrols are governed by five principles: planning, reconnaissance, security, control, and common sense. In brief, each principle involves:

Planning. Quickly make a simple plan and effectively communicate it to the lowest level. A great plan that takes forever to complete and is poorly disseminated is not a great plan. Plan and prepare to a realistic standard and rehearse everything.

Reconnaissance. Your responsibility as a leader is to confirm what you think you know, and to learn that which you do not already know.

Security. Preserve your force as a whole. Every teammate and every carbine counts, either one could be the difference between victory and defeat.

Control. Clarify the concept of the operation and commander's intent, coupled with disciplined communications, to bring every fighter and weapon available to overwhelm the enemy at the decisive point.

Common sense. Use all available information and good judgment to make sound, timely decisions.

Area Reconnaissance

What is it and when/why would we specify a mission as an Area Reconnaissance?

What it is. It is a form of reconnaissance that focuses on obtaining detailed information about the terrain, enemy or civilian activity within a prescribed area. An area may include a town, a ridgeline, section of woods, or any other critical feature (all of these are translated to NAIs by the planner). The area may only consist of a single structure such as a bridge or a building or it may be a larger well-defined area like a drive-in movie theater or a power station.

No matter the type of objective having a good PIR or set of PIRs is imperative. We don't send our team on half-planned unworkable missions. A PIR focused on the area around the facility makes sense while sending a four man team to recon the inside of the enemy occupied building is not realistic.

When/why we would use Area Recon. The leader would specify an area reconnaissance when the physical space/area he wants to collect on is somewhat defined and he or she knows where they want to focus the recon effort.

How we conduct Area Recon (overview). In an area reconnaissance, the patrol uses vantage points or observation posts around the objective to observe it and surrounding area. There are two ways of doing this, we can maneuver elements through the area or establish observation posts inside or external to the area of interest.

Actions at the objective for an area reconnaissance begin with the patrol in the ORP, and end with a dissemination of information after a linkup of the patrol's subordinate units. The critical actions include:

Actions from the ORP.

Execute the observation plan.

Link back up and continue the mission.

The patrol occupies the ORP and conducts associated priorities of work. While the patrol establishes security and prepares for the mission, the patrol leader and selected personnel conduct a leader's recon. During any of the missions discussed in this section use of the 5 Point Contingency Plan (discussed in CM-1, GOTWA) is critical. There will be no time or ability to communicate contingencies if things go wrong while the teams are dispersed on mission.

The leader must accomplish three things during this reconnaissance: pinpoint the objective and establish surveillance, identify a release point and follow-on linkup point (if required), and confirm the observation plan.

Observation Plan for an Area Reconnaissance

Upon returning from the leader's reconnaissance, the patrol leader disseminates information and FRAGOs as required. Once ready, the patrol departs. Once security is in position, the reconnaissance element moves along the specified routes to the observation posts and vantage points in accordance with the observation plan.

Long-range observation or surveillance is the observation of an objective from an OP. It must be far enough from the objective to be outside enemy small-arms range and its local security measures. This method is used whenever METT-TC permits the required information to be gathered from a distance. Long-range observation is the most desirable method for executing an area reconnaissance since the patrol does not come in close enough to be detected. Also, if the patrol is discovered, direct and indirect (if available) fires can be employed on the objective without endangering the patrol. When information cannot be gathered from one OP, successive OPs may be used. This is accomplished by squad-size reconnaissance patrols. The OPs must use available cover and concealment and have a good view of the objective.

Short-range observation or surveillance (close reconnaissance) is the act of watching an objective from a place that is within the range of enemy local security measures and small-arms fire. When information needed cannot be obtained by observing from a distance, the patrol moves closer to the objective. This method can be executed by the team or by a squad. The routes and area to be reconnoitered must be clearly defined and the teams have to have their stuff together. Saying this is a high risk approach is an understatement.

Security Element. The leader responsible for security (your HTL if you are operating a heavy squad) establishes security at the ORP and positions other security teams as required on likely enemy avenues of approach into the objective area while the RandS Teams are out on mission. Near the objective the patrol leader establishes a forward release point on the friendly side of the PLOC. It should be sited so it is well-hidden, no closer than 200 meters (for close recon) from known enemy patrol routes, observation posts, or sentry positions. The forward release point provides the patrol leader with a temporary location close to the objective from which he can operate. While the close reconnaissance is in progress, it should be manned by the assistant patrol leader and RTO. Only critical radio transmissions should be made while in the forward release point.

The close reconnaissance team should make its final preparation in the forward release point. Movement from the forward release point must be slow and deliberate. If the enemy position is large, or time is limited, the leader may employ more than one close reconnaissance team. If this occurs, each patrol must have clearly defined routes for movement to and from the forward release point. They also must have clearly defined areas in which to conduct their reconnaissance to avoid fratricide.

The close reconnaissance team normally consists of one to two observers and two security scouts. The security should be close enough to provide protection to the observer, but far enough away so his position is not compromised. When moving in areas close to the enemy position, only one man should move at a time. Bounds should be short; not that you are going to be using a handgun for this but think in terms of pistol range for the distances we are describing.

Once in position, the patrol observes and listens to acquire the needed information. If the reconnaissance element cannot acquire the information needed from its initial position, it backs off (retraces their initial route) and repeats the process in what resembles a cloverleaf from above. The team may use this "cloverleaf method" to get different vantage points or line of sight angles on the objective. This method of reconnaissance can be extremely risky, the closer the element is the greater the risk of being detected. Using binos, thermals, and NV systems to keep as much distance as possible between scouts and the objective while still being able to gather the required info is the sweet spot for us, we want to be doing long-range observation. You don't have to stand on an objective to recon it, your scouts should be experienced and know that more distance is better but sometimes you must get closer.

Area Recon overview; scouts cannot observe or answer PIR from OP1 so they have to move closer. Security teams are not depicted but will be present and able to support the recon team if they are compromised.

Multiple Reconnaissance and Surveillance Teams

When information cannot be gathered from just one observation post or vantage point, successive points may be used. Once determined, the leader decides how his patrol will occupy them. The critical decision is determining the number of teams in the reconnaissance element. The advantages of a single team are the leader's ability to control the team, and a decreased probability of enemy detection. The disadvantages of a single team are the lack of redundancy, and the objective area is observed with just one team. The advantages of using multiple teams include providing the leader redundancy in accomplishing his mission, and ability to look at the objective area from more than one perspective. The disadvantages include the increased probability of being detected by the enemy, and increased difficulty in controlling the teams. During the conduct of the reconnaissance, each R&S team returns to the RP when any of the following occurs: all their PIR is gathered, the LOA is reached, the allocated time to conduct the reconnaissance has elapsed, enemy contact is made.

At the RP, the leader analyzes what information has been gathered and determines if it meets the PIR requirements. If the leader determines that insufficient information to meet the PIR requirements has been gathered, or if the information he and the subordinate leader gathered differs drastically, R&S teams may be sent back to the objective site. In this case, R&S teams alternate areas of responsibilities. For example, if one team reconnoitered from the 6–3–12, then that team now reconnoiters from the 6–9–12 o'clock side of the OBJ.

The R&S element then returns undetected to the ORP by the specified time and disseminates information to all patrol members through key leaders, or moves to a position at least one terrain feature or one kilometer away to disseminate. The patrol leader has the RTO (or BICC if not the RTO) prepare three sketches of the objective site based on the leader's sketch and provides copies to the subordinate leaders to assist in dissemination. The R&S element reports any information requirements or any information requiring immediate attention to your higher HQ, and departs for the designated area.

If contact is made, the compromised element returns a sufficient volume of fire to allow them to break contact. All elements pull off the objective and move to the RP. The senior leader quickly accounts for all personnel and returns to the ORP. It will be chaotic. The security team at the ORP must ensure they know where all friendlies are as the reconnaissance element tries to break contact and return to the ORP, secure rucksacks, and quickly move out of the area. Once they have moved a safe distance away, the leader informs higher HQ of the situation.

Security teams must ensure they know where all friendlies are if the recon element must break contact and return to the ORP. Running passwords, recognition signals, and situational awareness must be flawless. Train your teams to make decisions during the chaos of gunfire and armed friendlies running toward you to prevent fratricide.

Zone Reconnaissance

What is it and when/why would we specify a mission as a Zone Reconnaissance?

What it is. A Zone Recon is finding and reporting all enemy forces within the zone and reporting on terrain related PIR. Zone reconnaissance focuses on enemy, terrain, or civilian population and consider infrastructure a part of terrain. A zone is defined by an LD (linear graphic control measure) bounded laterally by unit boundaries. A quick TTP, good planners always name their boundaries as Phase Lines as well to build in flexibility. Think of unit boundaries somewhat like property lines, they are a unit's left and right limits. At the far end you will have another phase line that is designated as the Limit of Advance (LOA).

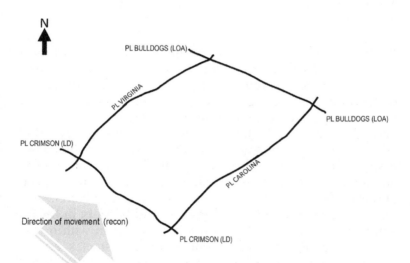

Rudimentary example of Zone Recon boundaries; unit will conduct Zone Recon from PL CRIMSON (LD) to PL BULLDOGS (LOA) between PL VIRGINIA and PL CAROLINA

The primary difference between an area and a zone reconnaissance is in an area recon units move to the area in which the reconnaissance will take place. In a zone reconnaissance, the units conducting the reconnaissance start from a line of departure and are assessing everything between the two lateral boundaries as they progress (this is why zone is time and resource consuming). Areas are smaller than zones and typically take less time to complete.

Compared to conventional force doctrine our zone reconnaissance is going to be different. We must make our zone recon requirements realistic for what we have; they must be less resource and time intensive and more averse to direct fire contact for all the reasons we have discussed in this manual.

For comparison's sake and to keep ourselves grounded in reality, here is a summary of the doctrinal tasks for a *conventional force zone reconnaissance*:

By doctrine when conducting a zone recon a conventional unit must (based on engagement criteria) clear all enemy forces in the designated AO within the capability of the unit conducting reconnaissance, determine the trafficability of all terrain in the zone (including urban/suburban areas), locate and determine the extent of all contaminated (hazmat or chemicals) areas in the zone, inspect and classify all bridges within the zone, locate river and stream fords or crossing sites within the zone, inspect and classify all overpasses, underpasses, and culverts, locate and clear all mines, obstacles, and barriers in the zone (within capability), reconnoiter all terrain within the zone, locate bypass around built-up area, obstacles, and contaminated areas. **This is quite a long task list for *any* organization to handle, much less the small types of units we have.** Once again, we must depart from accepted doctrine; we will still use the zone recon term but will adjust what it means in actual execution.

198

When/why we would use Zone Recon. As a small irregular force, we use zone reconnaissance to obtain detailed information on routes, obstacles, terrain, enemy forces, or specific civil considerations within a zone. These are selectively chosen so we don't overtask our unit. A zone reconnaissance is used when the enemy situation is vague or when information related to terrain, infrastructure, or society is limited (if you are operating in an unfamiliar area). We also conduct zone recons when information becomes "stale"; this when we assess a piece of information has had the opportunity to change since we last looked at it (eg since the heavy rain is the unimproved road and the side trails in zone passable by 2wd vehicles?).

How we conduct Zone Recon (overview). The level of detail required during a zone reconnaissance makes these operations a deliberate and time-consuming process even if we reduce the number of "things" we are looking at compared to that conventional force task list we talked about before. The patrol leader must work to balance available time with critical collection requirements to ensure that they provide the necessary information for the higher unit commander (or themselves if it is a self-directed mission). Property patrols will most likely fall into the zone recon category for us as these have elements of a Security Patrol and Zone Recon, but with the lack of combat power they are aligned very well with the modified understanding of a zone recon. We will be familiar with the terrain, so we are out deliberately looking for presence of enemy forces, criminal activity, signs of trespass, or maybe a change in a familiar piece of ground (river flood status, storm damage, fire break condition etc).

When the reconnaissance objective is the enemy force, a leader may omit a detailed recon of the zone and focus assets on those named areas of interest that would reveal enemy dispositions. A recon unit cannot disregard terrain altogether when focusing on the enemy, however, it limits

its terrain reconnaissance to the components that may influence the named areas of interest you are focused on.

Zone reconnaissance techniques include the use of moving elements, stationary teams, or can combine multiple area reconnaissance actions.

When speed is the primary concern, the leader or commander directing the mission will modify the focus, tempo, and engagement criteria to prioritize the tasks for the patrol leader. The leader will determine the width of the zone (the two side boundaries we discussed) and define it for the patrol leader by using the road network, terrain features, anticipated enemy activity, and time available to accomplish the mission. For a property patrol this concept may apply as well, coordinating with neighbors to ensure you have freedom of maneuver to expand lateral boundaries based on terrain and not the county property plat. You may need to check areas that are not on your property but have observation and fields of fire into your AO due to the line of sight. Unmanned assets can be used to observe areas beyond the reach of ground reconnaissance elements, caution is always in order to manage the electronic and noise signature.

To maximize reconnaissance assets and prepare for contact, the patrol leader deploys teams (gets them spread out in the prescribed formation and technique of movement) before reaching the LD. The patrol is in position early enough to conduct observation of the LD. To do this, the patrol leader designates a section or team to conduct a reconnaissance of the route from the SP to the release point (RP), and take note of the time it takes to complete the movement. This time is used in deciding when to execute the SP (important when synchronizing with adjacent scout units conducting a mission or timing to take advantage of a desired lighting condition), allowing the unit enough time to complete movement to the LD and establish initial observation posts.

Scouts conduct the zone reconnaissance by using the movement technique in the OPORD. There are three methods we will discuss, they are *Fan, Converging Routes, and Box (Successive Sector will not be addressed).* The patrol leader can choose any for a zone recon (remember we will not conduct the full zone recon tasks as an irregular force, but you can adapt these methods to fit your capabilities and situation). The security and observation techniques from the Area Recon still apply as the team moves through the zone.

Fan. The fan method uses a series (fan) of ORPs and each reconnaissance element moves from the ORP along a different fan-shaped route. Routes overlap with that of other reconnaissance to elements to ensure reconnaissance of the entire area. When all reconnaissance elements return to the ORP, the patrol leader collects and disseminates all information before moving to the next ORP in the zone.

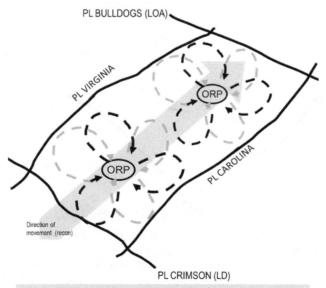

Zone Reconnaissance using the Fan Method

Converging Routes Method. The patrol leader selects routes from the ORP through zone to a rendezvous point at the far side of the zone from the ORP. Each reconnaissance element moves and reconnoiters along a specified route and then converge (linkup) at one time and place. The methods don't require a lot of explanation, they are just that – methods of doing the same task. The same foundational principles and individual / collective tasks remain (mostly) the same as the other methods.

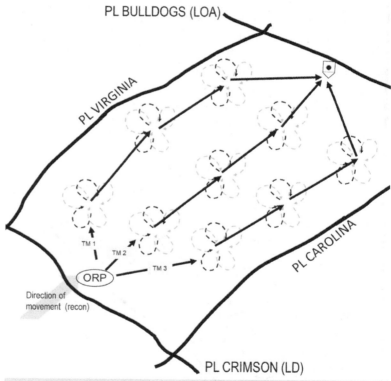

Zone Recon using the converging-routes method (which incorporates the fan method), select an ORP and reconnaissance routes through the zone and the rendezvous point.

Box Method. PL sends reconnaissance elements from the first ORP along routes that form a box (ok, it is a pseudo box, the idea is that the two flank team routes fully enclose the area if drawn on a map), and then sends other elements along routes throughout the box. All teams linkup at the far side of the box from the ORP.

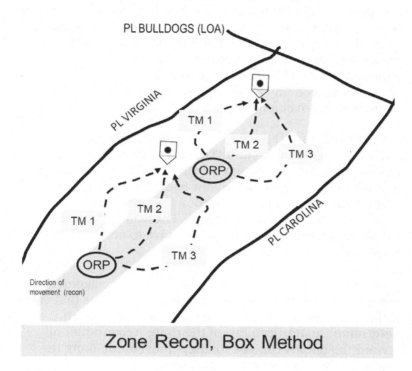

Zone Recon, Box Method

During the entire patrol, members continuously gain and exchange all information gathered, but cannot consider the mission accomplished unless all PIR has been gathered.

A patrol must be able to break contact and return to the friendly unit with what information is gathered. Leaders emplace security elements where they can overwatch the reconnaissance and if necessary, they will suppress the enemy so the reconnaissance element can break contact.

Route Reconnaissance

What it is. A route reconnaissance is a directed effort to obtain detailed information of a route and all terrain from which the enemy could influence that route. A full scout platoon normally conducts route reconnaissance due to the complexity and number of tasks. It is like the zone recon in the time and resource consuming list of requirements; the doctrinal task list is too long and involved for our needs or resources. Route recons answer questions for the commander about the presence and disposition of obstacles and enemy along a route and whether it will support the movement of friendly vehicles.

Just as we did for the zone, here is the route recon doctrinal task list for a unit. This list is so involved just reading this paragraph may be painful...imagine trying to execute all these tasks with your team. The learning point is the requirements are a heck of a lot more than what we would ever be able to accomplish. These are a "may have to" list in doctrine, tasks they may have to accomplish in a route reconnaissance.

These tasks are: find, report, and based on engagement criteria, clear within capabilities all enemy forces that can influence movement along the route. reconnoiter and determine the trafficability of the route, reconnoiter all terrain the enemy can use to affect movement along the route. reconnoiter all built-up areas along route, reconnoiter all lateral routes, conduct out-posting along lateral routes to identify potential enemy positions and forces that could influence the route. inspect and classify all bridges within the area, reconnoiter defiles along the route, clear of enemy and obstacles (within capability), or locate a bypass, inspect and classify all overpasses, underpasses, and culverts, locate fords or crossing sites near all bridges on the route, locate and clear all IEDs, mines, obstacles, and barriers on the route within capability.

Quite a task list wasn't it? We will still use the route recon term and associated principals, but you will adjust the tasks to fit your requirements. Bridge and route classifications alone are insanely complex so unless you have a civil engineer or a former heavy regiment cav scout in your midst you will most likely not have the expertise to do these. Unless you are part of a well-trained team you will not be conducting route and bridge classification, odds are most of our units will be at the foundational end of the route recon spectrum due to the required skillsets.

When/why we would use Route Recon. As a small irregular force, we use route reconnaissance to obtain detailed information on routes, obstacles, terrain, enemy forces, or specific civil considerations along a road. As you did with the zone recon you will focus on specific components of these so you don't overtask your unit while meeting the mission requirements. You may want to find out if the enemy has emplaced obstacles on the traditional routes through your AO. Are the bridges still intact so you can receive supplies from other regions? Have the roads been mined? You would use a route recon to determine where the best ambush points are along the route (both giving and receiving); always remember to look at terrain from both the friendly and enemy perspectives. A mounted recon unit is much better suited for this mission set, a dismounted scout unit conducting a route recon is a tough mission to say the least.

How we conduct Route Recon (overview). Sometimes when we are conducting a route recon we may become desensitized to the fact that they are still natural lines of drift, high speed enemy avenues of approach, linear and open danger areas. If we were moving across the same route during a patrol we would limit our exposure or avoid it altogether; and would be very concerned about being anywhere near it. In the case of a route recon we are deliberately associating with a linear danger area for extended periods of time. Don't take this as me saying we

205

are walking down the road the entire time, but just realize that even if we are on the flanks in the woodline we are still exposing ourselves to that danger by proximity.

The OPORD the patrol leader receives (or initially generates if this is self-directed) specifies the route he must reconnoiter and defines the route from SP (Start Point aka where the route begins) to RP (Release Point or where the route ends). These start and end points are not necessarily where a physical road starts and ends (it may be the case but not always); a route for our purposes is a graphic control measure used to identify a road. You may use a route recon to assess unimproved roads and even goat trails (See CM-1). Additionally, the order should specify unit boundaries, LD, and LOA or reconnaissance objective. These control measures specify how much terrain on both sides of the route the patrol must reconnoiter and where the operation must begin and end. The patrol needs to reconnoiter all lateral routes and terrain that can influence the route out to at least half the max effective range of their respective direct fire weapon system. It is easy to get carried away on laterals and go too far, the team must understand the risks and the patrol leader must manage those graphic control measures to make sure our team doesn't get beyond support distance.

During the initial planning phase, the patrol leader must take into consideration the type of vehicle movement the route reconnaissance is supporting. For example, if a patrol is conducting a route reconnaissance to determine the feasibility of serving as a main supply route for supply convoys, the patrol leader must understand what types of vehicles will utilize the route. We may be using UTVs / ATVs, pickup trucks, transfer trucks etc. Understanding the purpose of the route enables the patrol leader to develop NAI's specifically tied to curves, slopes, bridges, roadbed type and the effects of weather, and other terrain features.

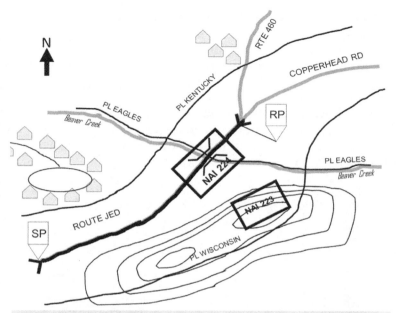

Basic Route Reconnaissance graphics (simplified) showing the Route to be reconnoitered (ROUTE JED) and two NAIs that will provide information for decision. NAI 223 might have a PIR "will the enemy have OPs along PL WISCONSIN observing the BEAVER CREEK crossing?" Based on your terrain analysis you know the high ground on the east side of the saddle is the most likely place for an enemy OP so you would place an NAI and recon it as part of the RTE JED Route Recon.

The patrol leader will build graphics to support the tasks that are required; multiple checkpoints, linkup points, OPs, ORPs...all the techniques and principles you know from the area and zone recon still apply. The route recon is one that may require boots on the actual objective depending on the information needed. You may have to get close to look for signs of buried mines, high strength wires strung across that are invisible at distance (used against our ATV/motorcycle riders), markings or pre-cuts for timber charge emplacements etc etc. You may have to send scouts under bridges and into culverts to see if they have been intentionally weakened or rigged for explosives. If we are supporting / scouting for a friendly force that is trying to deny usage of the route the same observations are taken, just from the other perspective...optimal ambush sites, where friendlies could roadblocks or abatis (a group of trees deliberately cut down to block a passage). There are no canned or prescribed solutions, only principles, common language and terms, and sound recon tactics. Reconnaissance is a thinking person's game, tactically sound creativity is what this is all about.

Reconnaissance is a thinking person's game; tactically sound creativity is what this is all about.

Conclusion

So that is a lot to take in and learn isn't it? We didn't delve too far into TLPs, the detailed orders process, or even address passage of lines, actions on contact / battle drills, secondary weapons, or urban operations. The foundational contact drills are in CM-1, always keep those in mind as you digest this manual's contents. The CM series of manuals is intended to be a library of interrelated material, every manual in the series is and will be inter-related.

We will get to more of the detailed patrolling tasks (crossing danger areas, patrol base operations, raids, ambushes, urban etc) in later manuals, but this is enough for the reader to take on and learn from the second book in the series. Practice these individual Scout skills and techniques, get your small teams and squads maneuvering together. More to follow in the series, we will continue to write and push reference quality content out for you. Thanks again for your support for The Professional Citizen Project!

Glossary - Terms, Acronyms, Abbreviations, and a few limited Definitions

AAR
After Action Review

ACE
Ammo, Casualties, Equipment (sometimes reported as LACE, L being Liquids); also the CM-9 manual Adverse Conditions and Environments

BMNT
Begin Morning Nautical Twilight

Buddy Team of Scout Team
Two (or three if there is an odd man out) inseparable battle buddies. Implemented for accountability, buddy team rushes/maneuver, and well-being of the unit.

CM
Citizen Manual

Combat Ineffective
The status of a unit or individual when they become physically or mentally unable to perform assigned warfighting tasks

COTS
Commercial Off The Shelf; referring to an item that is available for free market purchase

Destruction Plan
Pre determined actions to prevent the imminent capture of sensitive friendly equipment or information

EENT
End Evening Nautical Twilight

Fire Team
A group of fighters led by a Team Leader (TL), can be three or four individuals with assigned roles and potentially various weapon systems/capabilities (doctrine is four consisting of TL, Automatic Rifleman, Grenadier and Rifleman)

Fire Team Leader
Leads the smallest maneuver element, typically leads three individuals but can be up to 5

FMC
Fully Mission Capable

FRAGO
Fragmentary Order (current doctrine is "FRAGORD", but we will still use FRAGO)

Guerrilla Force
A group of irregular, predominantly indigenous personnel organized along military lines to conduct military and paramilitary operations in enemy-held, hostile, or denied territory.

HSW
Heavy Support Weapon, a 7.62x51 magazine fed weapon with a magnified optic used for additional suppression by precision and volume (limited volume)

HTL
Heavy Team Leader, leads the third team in a heavy squad

IPB Intelligence preparation of the battlefield/battlespace
A systematic process of analyzing the mission variables of enemy, terrain, weather, and civil considerations in an area of interest to determine their effect on operations

LMG
Light Machine Gun

LSW
Light Support Weapon, a magazine fed heavy barrel carbine or rifle with a magnified optic

MIFAK (pronounced as "my-fack")
Minor Injury/Illness First Aid Kit (what some call a "boo boo kit"

NLT
Not Later Than

OPORD
Operation Order (sometimes referenced as "Operations Order")

Resistance Movement
An organized effort by some portion of the civil population of a country to resist the legally established government or an occupying power and to disrupt civil order and stability.

Scout Carbine
A lightweight 5.56 carbine capable of passive NV engagements optimized for a Scout

Squad
A group of fighters led by a Squad Leader (SL), can be seven to thirteen individuals organized into two or three fire teams with assigned roles and potentially various weapon systems/capabilities (Army doctrine is nine men consisting of a SL, 2x TL, 2x Automatic Rifleman, 2x Grenadier and 2x Rifleman)

SOP
Standard Operating Procedure (or Standing)

SPOTREP
Spot Report, use SALUTE format

STANAG
standardization agreement (NATO)

Tactical Bushcraft
Expanded fieldcraft skills that enhance the ability to survive without external support; bushcraft type skills that are tailored for and adhere to the requirements of a tactical environment.

WARNO
Warning Order (current doctrine is "WARNORD", this change has been determined as unnecessary, so we still use WARNO)

WP
white phosphorus (aka "Willie Pete" refers to smoke or weapon), also means white phosphor in context (referring to night vision)

X Hour
Term we use to designate the moment when a crisis event kicks off.

ANNEX A STANDARD REPORT FORMATS

SPOT REPORT (SPOTREP, SALUTE Report format)

This is sometimes referred to as a "BLUE 1" Report. Lines can be used (Alpha, Bravo etc) but that is up to your group and local SOP.

Line ALPHA: Observer or source (omit if it is the calling station, otherwise use call signs or description).

Line BRAVO: Activity or characteristic observed. Use the SALUTE format:

Size: The number of sighted personnel, vehicles, or other equipment.
Activity: What the threat is doing.
Location: Grid coordinates. Report the center of mass for identical, closely grouped items,
otherwise, report multiple grid coordinates of traces.
Unit: Patches, signs, or markings.
Time: Time the observed activity occurred.
Equipment: Description or identification of all equipment associated with the activity.

Line CHARLIE: Actions you have taken and personal recommendations. Actions usually involve conducting additional reconnaissance to determine the complete threat situation or recommending and executing a specific course of action.

Line DELTA: Self-authentication (if required by SOP or tactical situation).

SITUATION REPORT (SITREP)

(This is sometimes referred to as a "BLUE 2" Report) Subordinate units submit a SITREP on the tactical situation and status to their leadership or command post. Submit the SITREP daily (follow your SOP), after significant events, or when the leadership requests it. State SITREP followed by pertinent information on these lines:

Line 1: The as-of date-time group (DTG).

Line 2: Brief summary of threat activity, casualties inflicted, and prisoners captured.

Line 3: Friendly locations (encoded, follow unit SOP)

Line 4: Number of operational vehicles (if applicable).

Line 5: Defensive (friendly) obstacles (encoded using codes, control measures, or TIRS points). These may include debris or abatis roadblocks you have emplaced, wire obstacles etc.

Line 6: Personnel strength classified using the following status levels:
      GREEN: Full strength; 90% or more fit for combat.
      AMBER: Reduced strength; 80% to 89% fit for combat.
      RED: Reduced strength; 60% to 79% fit for combat; the unit is mission capable.
      BLACK: Reduced strength; 59% or less fit for combat.

Line 7: Water, Ammo, and food supplies available. Status levels for ammunition and etc are the same ones used for personnel strength (GREEN, AMBER, RED, or BLACK) with percentages referring to the amount of basic load level available. (Refer to Line 6 of this report.)

Line 8: Summary of tactical intentions.

OBSTACLE REPORT (also referred to as a BLUE 9 report).

This is used to report threat or unknown emplaced obstacles to other friendly units or your leadership. Report all pertinent information using the following format:

Line ALPHA: Type of obstacle or obstruction.

Line BRAVO: Location, using grid coordinates. For large, complex obstacles, send the coordinates of the ends and all turn points.

Line CHARLIE: Dimensions and orientation.

Line DELTA: Composition.

Line ECHO: Threat weapons influencing obstacle.

Line FOXTROT: Observer's actions.

Bypass Report also referred to as a Blue 10 report).

Report all pertinent information using the following format:

(1) Line ALPHA: Observer or source.

(2) Line BRAVO: Length; width; surface type; grade (percent if known).

(3) Line CHARLIE: Coordinates of "from"/"to" locations. Eg a wire obstacle or fence end points

(4) Line DELTA: Seasonal/weather limitations.

(5) Line ECHO: Bypass markings.

(6) Line FOXTROT: Observer's actions; what you are doing and what do you recommend

ANNEX B
Classes of Supply

You may hear these referenced in the community, get familiar with what each denotes as they will appear in military manuals. For example "what is your Class Five status?" is asking what the ammo status is in your unit.

Class I
Subsistence, water, and gratuitous health and comfort items

Class II
Clothing, individual equipment, tentage, organizational tool sets, hand tools, unclassified maps, administrative and housekeeping supplies and equipment, and chemical, biological, radiological, and nuclear (CBRN) equipment

Class III
Petroleum (bulk and packaged), oils, and lubricants

Class IV
Construction fortification and barrier materiel

Class V
Ammunition

Class VI
Personal demand items normally sold through exchanges

Class VII
Major end items

Class VIII
Medical materiel, including repair parts peculiar to medical equipment

Class IX
Repair parts and components

ANNEX C
The Nine Person Squad ("A" way)

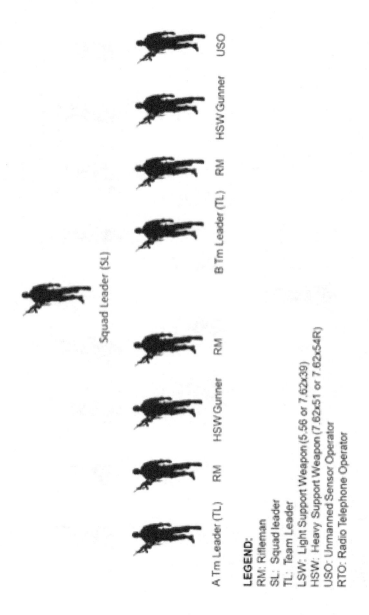

Squad Leader (SL)

A Tm Leader (TL)   RM   HSW Gunner   RM   B Tm Leader (TL)   RM   HSW Gunner   USO

LEGEND:
RM: Rifleman
SL: Squad leader
TL: Team Leader
LSW: Light Support Weapon (5.56 or 7.62x39)
HSW: Heavy Support Weapon (7.62x51 or 7.62x54R)
USO: Unmanned Sensor Operator
RTO: Radio Telephone Operator

219

ANNEX D
Heavy Squad ("A" way)

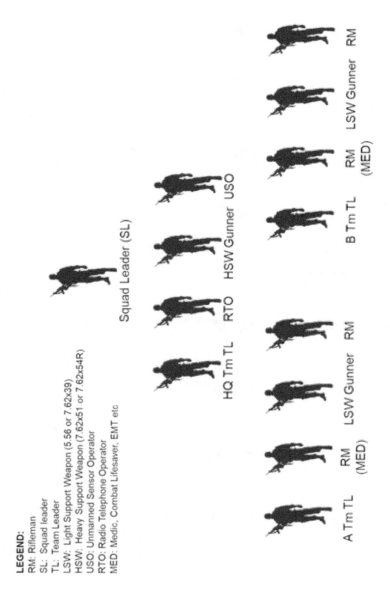

LEGEND:
RM: Rifleman
SL: Squad leader
TL: Team Leader
LSW: Light Support Weapon (5.56 or 7.62x39)
HSW: Heavy Support Weapon (7.62x51 or 7.62x54R)
USO: Unmanned Sensor Operator
RTO: Radio Telephone Operator
MED: Medic, Combat Lifesaver, EMT etc

Squad Leader (SL)

HQ Tm TL · RTO · HSW Gunner USO

A Tm TL · RM (MED) · LSW Gunner · RM

B Tm TL · RM (MED) · LSW Gunner · RM

ANNEX E Reverse Planning Timeline Shell

Reverse Planning Timeline

TIME ANALYSIS
Usable Light versus Limited Light

MINUS:

Receipt of order/Movement _____ Hours
Higher Unit TLPS _____ Hours

THE PROFESSIONAL
Total CITIZEN PROJECT _____ Hours — + — ➤

☐ Daylight   ▥ NVG Window

▨ Limited Visibility   ■ Darkness

Total Time Until LD ___ Hours
⌈ Daylight ___ Hours ⌉
⌊ Limited Light ___ Hours ⌋

Minus ___ Hours

Total Time Available ___ Hours

1/3 – 2/3 = OPORD NLT _____
1/5 – 4/5 = OPORD NLT _____

ANNEX F
OP Placement Example (enlargement of page 98)

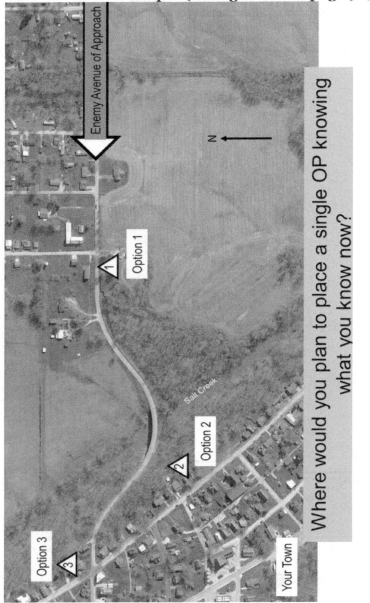

Enemy Avenue of Approach

Option 1

Option 2

Option 3

Salt Creek

Your Town

N

Where would you plan to place a single OP knowing what you know now?

☒ Option 1 – Good line of sight down the hardball road, but the OP is exposed to the enemy and potentially out of direct fire support range from the friendly positions (in town). Most importantly the Scouts in that OP have their backs to a river with only a single exposed crossing point. **NO GO**

☒ Option 2 – Can observe the bridge crossing sight along the avenue of approach. Very limited line of sight to the East, they can see the bridge but there is a missed opportunity to see the enemy earlier (eg farther East). Close enough for wire comms (field phone) or even hand / visual signals. Option 2 is OK, but it is not not the best option for us.

☑ Option 3 – Scouts have the same line of sight as option 1 but aren't trapped on the wrong side of the river. They can detect a threat long before they get to the bridge. OP3 has good escape routes back into the town without being exposed to the east, close enough use field phone/wire comms, great line of sight, and keeps an existing obstacle between them and the majority of the threat. Option 3 is the best option (this is a simplified discussion of course; far more factors will come into play for you on the ground for real).

223

References

ADRP 1-02. *Terms and Military Symbols*, 7 December 2015.

JP 1-02. *Department of Defense Dictionary of Military and Associated Terms*, 8 November 2010.

ADP 5-0. *The Operations Process*, 17 May 2012.

ADP 6-0. *Mission Command*, 17 May 2012.

ADRP 3-0. *Unified Land Operations*, 16 May 2012.

ADRP 3-07. *Stability*, 31 August 2012.

ADRP 3-09. *Fires*, 31 August 2012.

ADRP 3-90. *Offense and Defense*, 31 August 2012.

ADRP 5-0. *The Operations Process*, 17 May 2012.

ADRP 6-0. *Mission Command*, 17 May 2012.

ATP 2-01. *Plan Requirements and Assess Collection*, 19 August 2014.

ATP 2-01.3. *Intelligence Preparation of the Battlefield/Battlespace*, 10 November 2014.

ATP 3-20.98. *Reconnaissance Platoon*, 5 April 2013.

ATP 3-34.81. *Engineer Reconnaissance*, 1 March 2016.

ATP 3-53.2. *Military Information in Conventional Operations*, 7 August 2015.

FM 3-90-2. *Reconnaissance, Security, and Tactical Enabling Tasks Volume 2*, 22 March 2013.

FM 3-98. *Reconnaissance and Security Operations*, 1 July 2015.

FM 4-95. *Logistics Operations*, 1 April 2014.

FM 6-0. *Commander and Staff Organization and Operations*, 5 May 2014.

JP 3-0. *Joint Operations*, 11 August 2011.

JP 3-05. *Special Operations*, 16 July 2014.

Thank you for your support for the Professional Citizen Project!

Check out our other manuals and references in the series. We will continue to add to the list, please check our website and our social media accounts for the latest titles.

TheProCitizen.com

Citizen Manual 1, Individual Tactical Skills
by Jack Morris

Citizen Manual 2, Reconnaissance
by Jack Morris

Citizen Manual 9, Adverse Conditions and Environment (the ACE)
by Jay Pallardy (The Modern Minuteman)

Made in the USA
Middletown, DE
10 September 2024